Making Nonprofit N

Making Nonprofit News examines the essence of nonprofit journalism on multiple levels of analysis, explaining how individuals, routines, organizational makeup and outside institutions all affect news production at nonprofit news organizations.

The book argues that the market model itself – not simply the journalism industry – impacts news workers, news content and outside influence on the organization. Essentially, nonprofit journalism organizations are influenced by forces consistently impacting the industry as well as those previously not involved in journalism. Drawing on three years of in-depth interviews with more than 30 journalists at nonprofits, site visits and more broad research on nonprofit journalism, this book is a sociological study of how nonprofit status affects journalistic work. The book further conceptualizes the forces impacting newswork and examines the social institutions now on the boundaries of journalism due to their connection to nonprofit journalism.

Exploring how nonprofit news is disrupting the industry's very idea of news, news values and news processes, this is a helpful text for academics and researchers with an interest in journalism, media industries, media sociology and not-for-profits.

Patrick Ferrucci is an Assistant Professor and Associate Chair for Graduate Studies in the Department of Journalism in the College of Media, Communication and Information at the University of Colorado-Boulder. He holds a bachelors in sociology from Providence College, a masters in journalism from Emerson College and a Ph.D. focusing on media sociology from School of Journalism at the University of Missouri.

Disruptions: Studies in Digital Journalism
Series editor: Bob Franklin

Disruptions refers to the radical changes provoked by the affordances of digital technologies that occur at a pace and on a scale that disrupts settled understandings and traditional ways of creating value, interacting and communicating both socially and professionally. The consequences for digital journalism involve far reaching changes to business models, professional practices, roles, ethics, products and even challenges to the accepted definitions and understandings of journalism. For Digital Journalism Studies, the field of academic inquiry which explores and examines digital journalism, disruption results in paradigmatic and tectonic shifts in scholarly concerns. It prompts reconsideration of research methods, theoretical analyses and responses (oppositional and consensual) to such changes, which have been described as being akin to 'a moment of mind-blowing uncertainty'.

Routledge's new book series, *Disruptions: Studies in Digital Journalism*, seeks to capture, examine and analyse these moments of exciting and explosive professional and scholarly innovation which characterize developments in the day-to-day practice of journalism in an age of digital media, and which are articulated in the newly emerging academic discipline of Digital Journalism Studies.

Analyzing Analytics
Disrupting Journalism One Click at a Time
Edson C. Tandoc Jr.

Facebook, the Media and Democracy
Big Tech, Small State?
Leighton Andrews

Making Nonprofit News
Market Models, Influence and Journalistic Practice
Patrick Ferrucci

Conceptualizing Immersive Journalism
Ana Luisa Sánchez Laws

For more information, please visit: www.routledge.com/Disruptions/book-series/DISRUPTDIGJOUR

Making Nonprofit News
Market Models, Influence and Journalistic Practice

Patrick Ferrucci

Routledge
Taylor & Francis Group

LONDON AND NEW YORK

First published 2020 by Routledge

2 Park Square, Milton Park, Abingdon, Oxon OX14 4RN
605 Third Avenue, New York, NY 10017

Routledge is an imprint of the Taylor & Francis Group, an informa business

First issued in paperback 2022

Publisher's Note

The publisher has gone to great lengths to ensure the quality of this reprint
but points out that some imperfections in the original copies may be apparent.

British Library Cataloguing-in-Publication Data
A catalogue record for this book is available from the British Library

Library of Congress Cataloging-in-Publication Data
A catalog record has been requested for this book

ISBN: 978-0-367-20641-3 (hbk)
ISBN: 978-1-03-233803-3 (pbk)
DOI: 10.4324/9780429262661

Typeset in Times New Roman
by Wearset Ltd, Boldon, Tyne and Wear

For Owen... the best disruption a guy could ask for

Contents

Preface

Acknowledgments and reflections

In September of 2009, I was working as a music writer and arts and entertainment editor for the *New Haven Register* in New Haven, Connecticut. At the time, I would guess, my beer-league softball season was coming to an end (presumably badly since we didn't repeat as champions) and I was seriously thinking about going back to school for a Ph.D. I'm not sure if those two things are connected, but you never know.

After graduating from Providence College as an undergrad, I often thought about returning to school for a Ph.D., but while I knew I wanted to research something that connected journalism and sociology, I didn't realize what. Little did I know, though, that my scheduled trip to Columbia, Missouri, to visit the School of Journalism at the University of Missouri during that early part of September 2009 would coincide with an event that would shape my research agenda. You see, on September 8, 2009, a guy named Raymond Clark – a guy whose team my softball team played against at some point – murdered Annie Le, a doctoral student at Yale University's School of Medicine. Clark killed Le and stuffed her in a wall in a lab on Yale's campus in New Haven. Her body wasn't found until September 13, the day she planned to get married.

Murder. A wedding. Workplace violence. The Ivy League.

Put all those factors together and you get a media circus. A national frenzy overtook New Haven, with reporters getting injured at press conferences due to congestion, and folks like CNN infotainment talking head Nancy Grace taking turns shouting inaccurate garbage all over cable news. In short, the Annie Le murder generated more coverage than one can imagine. When I got to the University of Missouri's School of Journalism for my visit, people there asked me about it constantly whenever I mentioned I lived in New Haven. Now, keep in mind, around that time period, New Haven topped or came close to topping almost all lists of cities with the most murders per capita in the United States. I'd never been asked about any other murder in New Haven. And I'd never seen any other murder in New Haven receive so much national attention. Let's just say it was odd for national media to swarm the Elm City.

As a music writer, I took no part in coverage, but I watched it all. In New Haven, my paper covered the heck out of the story. The *Register* aimed for the best local coverage of one the biggest stories of the past couple decades. We didn't have much competition in the city, but the one other local place really dedicating resources to the investigation was the *New Haven Independent*, a digitally native news nonprofit founded in 2005 by a well-known local journalist named Paul Bass. Until Annie Le, most folks at the *Register* didn't think twice about the *Independent*. In fact, I only remember the organization mentioned once in a news meeting between 2005 and 2009 and that was when the *Register*'s great editor at the time, Jack Kramer, wondered if we should buy the nonprofit.

From my desk in the far corner of the newsroom, in between editing copy and writing about national and local music, I followed the coverage from both my paper and the *Independent*. We employed some absolutely great police writers, folks I consider amazing journalists. But it didn't take long to notice that our coverage differed from the *Independent*'s. Oh, sure, both places reported on all the new particulars leaking consistently, but our paper printed what I thought to be odd details: The name of the suspect's fiancé, the address of his parents, some random unsubstantiated rumors ... even the name of the suspect before police arrested him. The *Independent* did none of this.

I simply couldn't understand why. I knew that if you talked to the journalists from each organization and asked them about their goals or ethics, they would say similar things, but the coverage said something else. What was it about being for-profit vs. nonprofit that made such a difference, I wondered?

That question basically set the stage for my entire research agenda concerning how market models affect news production. Heck, the first solo-authored piece I ever published actually compares, through textual analysis, the differences in Annie Le coverage between the *Register* and *Independent*. That question, in a sense, guides this book, which attempts to identify all the factors and forces emanating from nonprofit status influencing newswork.

Of course, even with a book as short as this one, maybe one name graces the cover, but many names made this a reality. So many people have helped, both directly and indirectly, with the research that went into this book. This work puts together research I've done starting in 2011. I did the final interview for this book in 2019. So, yeah, a lot of people helped during that time and before. This starts, fittingly, with Erin Schauster, my favorite colleague at work and at home, whose support helps me be the best person I can. Also, to my parents, Paul and Diane Ferrucci, who chose to, you know, make me. A guy could not ask for more supportive folks. I'd also like to thank my brother, Nick Ferrucci, and his family, Brooke and Ethan Thibeault. Also, during the very early part of this research in St. Louis, my in-laws John and Michele Schauster let me bother them, I'm sure, by staying in their guest room

I kind of stumbled into journalism; I never wanted to be a journalist until I became one. When someone told me they'd pay me to write about music, I couldn't resist. Therefore, many people helped me become a decent journalist, which now helps me understand journalism. I want to specifically mention Rick Sandella, my boss (and, to this day, great friend) in New Haven who put in countless hours molding me from a good writer with a few years of journalism to experience to an actual journalist. At the University of Missouri, many professors and fellow grad students helped me go from a dude who knew nothing about research to a guy who knew at least something. Specifically, professors Earnest Perry, Stephanie Craft, Victoria Johnson, Glenn Leshner, Margaret Duffy and Esther Thorson spent a whole lot of time with me. When I arrived in Columbia in 2010, current PhD students such as Chad Painter and many others really helped me along. I was also fortunate to be part of the greatest cohort in the history of cohorts, a cohort that included my constant co-author, Edson Tandoc, who always makes me smarter, even if he always wears weird shirts with hearts on them. Of course, I would never have graduated and wouldn't have survived six years and counting as an assistant professor without the guidance of Tim Vos, a great advisor but, truly, a better friend.

I'd also like to thank my colleagues here at the University of Colorado-Boulder. I'm a dude who couldn't ask to work with smarter people who always make me better. Specifically, I've had two absolutely amazing chairs here in the Department of Journalism with Liz Skewes and Paul Voakes, and a dean in Lori Bergen who couldn't be more supportive. All of my colleagues have been consistently amazing and supportive, but I want to specifically mention Toby Hopp, Mike McDevitt, Jolene Fisher, Chris Vargo, Erin Willis, Ross Taylor, Tom Yulsman, Brian Quinn, Tim Kuhn, Reece Auguiste, Glenn Griffin and, of course, again, Erin Schauster … folks who make my days better and have taught me quite a bit. I've also had the pleasure of working with some kick-ass grad students here, but three of my advisees specifically helped with work directly associated with this book: Gayle Brisbane (now at Cal State-Fullerton), Angelica Kalika and Katie Alaimo. I'd also like to mention colleagues from other universities who've really helped me over the years in various ways. I'll mention by name Matt Carlson, who's always been a great mentor and incredibly generous with his time. And

David Wolfgang, Joy Jenkins, Valerie Belair-Gagnon and Jake Nelson, who've been great friends and sounding boards. Jake even read an early version of this manuscript for me. Also, at Routledge, I'd like to thank Jennifer Vennall and Margaret Farrelly, who consistently answered any questions I asked. I'm missing too many names, but this is already too long. My acknowledgments could be longer than the book ...

Seriously, I also want to take a moment to mention the editor of this book series, Bob Franklin. I've only met Bob in person once, at an ICA a handful of years ago. But I can't explain or overemphasize how supportive he's been through my time in academia. As the founding editor of *Journalism Studies*, *Journalism Practice* and *Digital Journalism*, Bob both accepted and rejected plenty of my studies, and always did so with such clear insight and warmth, something you don't really find all that often in academia. Bob's guidance throughout the writing and brainstorming of this book helped tremendously. In general, the world needs more people like Bob.

Finally, I want to thank all the journalists who gave me their time for this book and all the studies I self-cite. Over the last three or four years, I've interviewed more than 100 journalists, done fieldwork at various organizations and picked the brain of many on the boundaries of journalism. These people go to work every day, in a time when the press is unfairly and constantly ridiculed and do a hell of a job for not much money, all for the right to deliver needed information to the public. Lastly, for real, I want to especially mention *St. Louis Beacon* founder and editor Margaret Wolf Freivogel, who really shaped how I understand nonprofit journalism and personifies, I believe, the many journalists across the country working at nonprofits because of their belief in the power of news to make the world a better place.

1   Going nonprofit

An education reporter paces around the newsroom. It goes on for more than 20 minutes; he does not seem to ever consider stopping.

It's a Thursday afternoon during a particularly snowy winter in a large Midwestern city. The reporter paces around the spacious yet unpopulous newsroom literally talking to himself as he waits for a source to call him back. He's also awaiting word from his editor-in-chief concerning whether his expected story can run that day. The reporter, in his 50s, began covering various aspects of this city more than three decades ago and, on and off, covered education for more than two. He's carefully cultivated sources on the education beat for, as he says, "longer than some reporters doing the same job have been alive." Earlier on this afternoon, the reporter found out that the dean of a law school at a local university would be removed from his post due to sexual harassment. At the time, this university seemed to continuously encounter scandals and negative publicity. The reporter explained his progress to the editor by saying, "It's what we call a multi-layered story. I have all the bottom levels but nothing from the top. I have all the details but nothing confirmed and no idea what's real or not. I believe it all, but I'm reaching out to lots of sources to get confirmation." While the editor feels very confident that his story is accurate, she remains in no rush to get the story out. "I know this is an important and potentially big one," said the editor, "but we need to be right." She went on to note that being first would be good, but it's not vital.

About four hours later, another news outlet tweets that the university fired the dean. But almost immediately, the university denies the news. The reporter is still frantically making calls. "Maybe (the tweeting reporter) trusts his sources more than I do?" the reporter asks to nobody in particular. After a day passes, other outlets report the news of the firing, but the reporter holds back. He finally gets the confirmation he desired and the news organization publishes an article with far more context than any competitor. It comes a day late, though. Recalling the incident roughly two weeks later, the reporter discussed his frustration with not being first on the story:

> What really got me that day when I was making all the phone calls, and you were sitting right next to me and could see how frustrated it was getting me, was when I talked to the one professor who said to me, "OK, here are names and the email addresses of the two students who made these charges." And (the students) came back to me and said, "No, we didn't do it." But I knew that wasn't accurate.

This reporter was now working for a digitally native news nonprofit, a web-only news organization started by a group of former employees from the city's large metro newspaper. He'd also spent decades at said newspaper, but he was still getting used to the idea of not prioritizing breaking news. "It's about balancing being right and being first," he said. "If I was still at (my old newspaper), it would have really bothered me (to not be first) when I know I had the story first."

Implicit in the reporter's quotes, actions and the direction of the editor is the different way this particular nonprofit news organization set priorities. While other for-profit organizations in the city, staffed by education reporters with far less experience, ran with the story before it could be confirmed by the university, this nonprofit did not. In fact, it published a story almost 12 hours after all its competitors, but that story featured more than double the word count of any others, contextualized the issue in light of all the other negative incidents on campus and provided readers with more direct quotes from affected sources. In today's journalism, studies have illustrated the industry's thirst for breaking news, how most journalism organizations prioritize being first and "the 'newness of news' regardless of its drama or its significance."[1] This focus on breaking news is nothing new to journalism as early ethnographies of journalism practice also found organizations expending resources in their drive for scoops.[2] But the practice is becoming more and more ubiquitous in today's newsrooms as there remains a belief that breaking news could lead to more profit.[3]

Theoretically, however, nonprofit news organizations would not emphasize economic capital in the same way as a for-profit news enterprise. In the case of the previously mentioned education reporter, he was comparing working at a nonprofit entirely funded through foundation grants, nonprofit grants and public donations with working at his prior newspaper, one owned by a publicly traded media conglomerate. Throughout his career, the reporter received so much socialization in terms of the need to be first, that even though he internally knew the nonprofit did not care about such things and his editor reiterated that stance, he still could not ignore his thought that being first is a normative journalistic goal. "In the end, we delivered a quality story," he reasoned, "but if I could have just got that story out first, it would have been a double jackpot."

That story is just one anecdote illustrating how the rise in nonprofit journalism organizations across the United States is altering long-standing normative practices. Unburdened from the need to deliver profits to shareholders, nonprofit journalists are being asked to deviate from certain routines often embedded in newswork. However, it's not just journalistic routines that are changing at nonprofits: Due to the organizational structure of these newsrooms, many different influences impact the content eventually published.[4]

To better understand how these digital nonprofits engage in newswork, this book is the first piece of research to examine, in totality, the influences on news construction processes at digitally native news nonprofits. Foundational works of media sociology feature numerous ethnographies that found journalism organizations of the twentieth century often operated in a similar manner; essentially, the advertising-funded large newsrooms of previous eras were all, basically, influenced by same forces.[5] But digital nonprofits combine, among other factors, different funding structures, leadership hierarchies, physical spaces and technologies, and therefore potentially present a different combination of influences on newswork.

While the Associated Press began operating in 1846, many consider 1908 as the year, in the United States, when the first true modern mainstream nonprofit news organization published its first volume; more than 100 years ago, Mary Baker Eddy started *The Christian Science Monitor*, a newspaper that, to this day, operates with a stellar reputation in the journalism industry.[6] Yet, for almost a century, the *Monitor*, along with other like-minded news nonprofits such as National Public Radio, *Mother Jones* and the *St. Petersburg Times*, operated with very few contemporaries: The news ecology consisted of primarily advertising-driven news organizations that functioned with little, if any, competition from other market models.[7]

Yet, in the first two decades of the Internet era, especially since the turn of the century, the mainstream news media and professional journalism witnessed a disruption: No longer does one market model dominate the industry.[8] And one new market model that continues to see a steady increase in numbers and influence over the news industry is the digitally native news nonprofit; since 2004, the number of news nonprofits has grown from single digits to the hundreds.[9] Due to the influx of news nonprofits, journalism studies and media studies scholars have examined the market model in numerous manners such as how this model utilizes technology; how journalists conceptualize their role at these institutions; how the model is funded; how content differs compared from for-profit competition; how foundings are a response to layoffs at legacy media, how norms shift at these new organizations, or how nonprofits engage the audience. But despite a book detailing what digitally native news nonprofits idealistically could accomplish,[10] and one focusing extensively on nonprofits practicing investigative journalism,[11] no work systematically examines how going nonprofit impacts newswork.

While there are more than 1,000 public radio stations and more than 300 public television stations operating around the United States, this book concerns itself with a new breed of nonprofit: The digitally native news nonprofit. For decades, public radio and television in the United States have existed as underfunded and underutilized, and while this author agrees with the argument for a robust public media system, this book focuses on digitally native nonprofit news that it is not directly subsidized by the government.[12] These organizations are typically funded from a combination of donations from the public, grants, advertising, corporate sponsorships and by hosting various live events for communities and deep-pocketed elites.[13] The majority of these organizations were founded by former print journalists who willingly left legacy journalism because they believed those models no longer effectively served communities and strengthened democracy.[14] Many trace the beginnings of a boon in digital news nonprofits to the success of *Voice of San Diego*, a nonprofit founded in 2004 that can boast an impact "disproportionate to its steadily growing but still relatively modest audience."[15] Since *Voice* first published online, similarly structured news organizations started in cities such as Minneapolis, Austin, Birmingham and New Haven, and even some in small rural towns such as Carbondale, Colorado.

This book utilizes the hierarchy of influences model to identity and analyze the different forces on newswork at digital nonprofits. This model "takes into account the multiple forces that simultaneously impinge on media and suggest how influence at one level may interact with that at another."[16] The model allows researchers to separate the world into levels of analysis that can be examined separately and together. These levels help to place journalistic work within the proper contexts. This book features chapters discussing influences at four specific levels of an analysis: The individual, the communication routines, the organizational and the social institution levels.[17] The individual level of analysis refers to the personal characteristics of the individuals involved in the news work. The communication routines level refers to practices and procedures across all organizations in the industry that guide individual journalists. The organizational level discusses factors that originate from specific organizations, such as newsroom policies and priorities. The social institutional level refers to forces from institutions outside the organization, such as governments, audiences and advertisers.[18]

Utilizing the hierarchy of influence model is an optimal way to structure this book since the scope of this work aims to understand how nonprofit journalism exists within a larger structural environment. Essentially, the model "locates the individual journalist within a web of organizational and ideological constraints" and helps to place the phenomena of interest within a structural context."[19] In the very early days of media sociology work, scholars often believed that agency over how news turned out the way it did belonged to the individual journalist. In fact, David Manning White's iconic study of "Mr. Gates" fundamentally argued just that; however, journalists make decisions amongst a litany of other influences, some explicit and some implicit, and the hierarchy of influences model "raises the important distinction between structure and agency" by allowing researchers the ability to understand the totality of newsmaking and how it happens within a constellation of inside and outside forces.[20] Therefore, by situating nonprofit journalism within the entirety of the current media ecosystem, this book can help to illustrate the forces influencing newsmaking at these organizations, both forces salient at all news organizations and those unique or different for nonprofits. This allows for an understanding that some forces are homogenous across the industry, while others arise due to the very structure of going nonprofit.[21] In a sense, separating the news-making process into these identified levels of analysis allows this book to deliver a more nuanced understanding of newsmaking at nonprofits, one that can isolate individual influences but also put them in the proper context of newsmaking as a whole. The model allows the researcher to understand "journalism through these levels of analysis (and) helps untangle many of the critiques of press performance, identify their implicit normative and theoretical assumptions, and suggest appropriate kinds of evidence."[22] As such, each level operates both independently and also dependently to influence news production. Therefore, this book is structured in a way to allow the reader an understanding of each level individually – Chapters 2–5 each focus on specific levels – and then all influences together as the final chapter encapsulates the whole of the manuscript and theorizes using the hierarchy of influences.

This book derives from almost a decade of research on digitally native news nonprofits. Some of the data are taken from an ethnographic study conducted in 2013. Some draw from a pair of studies that compared content from nonprofits and legacy media.[23] However, the vast majority of the research for this work occurred between 2015–2018. During those years, I conducted in-depth interviews with 37 journalists at digitally native news nonprofits. These interviews ranged from 46 minutes to 105 minutes with an average time of roughly 71 minutes. The 37 journalists worked, at the time of the interview, for 30 different digitally native non-profit news organizations. The 37 number does not include the more than a dozen journalists interviewed at the *St. Louis Beacon* (now *St. Louis Public Radio*) conducted while doing my dissertation in 2013, or the seven inter-views conducted with journalists at the *Sopris Sun* for a more recent study.[24]

These interviews come from a large, long-term process of data collec-tion I began in 2015 as an assistant professor at Bradley University in Peoria, Illinois. Beginning in the spring of that year, right before moving to Boulder, I conducted the first of more than 100 long-form interviews with digital journalists. Over the course of almost four years, I interviewed full-time digital journalists in the United States. I transcribed each of these interviews myself and they have formed the basis of several studies I've published over the last four years; many of those studies are cited here. Of those more than 100 interviews, as noted above, 37 were conducted with full-time journalists at digitally native news nonprofits. I recruited particip-ants from digitally native news nonprofits in two different manners. First, I accessed a list of all members of the Online News Association and a research assistant of mine collected emails from this list and then seg-mented those people into categories such as nonprofit journalists. I then sent individual recruiting emails to all of these potential participants with a description of the study (which was approved by an Institutional Review Board at two different universities). Second, I had a different research assistant (RA) go through the Institute for Nonprofit News' Member Directory.[25] Once we removed member organizations not considered digit-ally native news nonprofits (for example, *Mother Jones*), my RA then went to each individual website and collected publicly available email addresses. These people then received the same recruitment email. Before I con-ducted any of these interviews, I made sure that the potential participant worked full time for their organization. While many of these nonprofit news organizations employ a significant amount of freelancers due to financial constraints and other reasons, because I wanted to focus on inside and outside influences, I believed full-time employees would have a much deeper and broader understanding of the organization. These emails all went out between 2015–2016. Since then, I individually recruited particip-ants, specifically focusing my recruitment on organizations not represented in the original recruitment period. This ongoing recruitment, post-2016, primarily focused on organizations that opened after 2015. I made sure not to include participants from an organization that had not published contin-uously for less than six months since I did not believe a brand-new organ-ization would have solidified its culture or way it operated. Table 1.1 shows a full list of organizations represented in this book.

Table 1.1 Interview subjects represented the following organizations (at the time of the interview)

Organization	Location
Aspen Journalism	Aspen, Colorado
Baltimore Brew	Baltimore, Maryland
Breckenridge Texan	Breckenridge, Texas
Center for Investigative Reporting	Berkeley, California
Chalkbeat	Chicago, Illinois
The City	New York, New York
CT Mirror	Hartford, Connecticut
Colorado Independent	Denver, Colorado
East Lansing Info	East Lansing, Michigan
Eye on Ohio	Cleveland, Ohio
Flint Beat	Flint, Michigan
Hartford Guardian	Hartford, Connecticut
Honolulu Civil Beat	Honolulu, Hawaii
InDepth NH	Lee, New Hampshire
Insider Louisville	Louisville, Kentucky
Iowa Center for Public Affairs Journalism	Iowa City, Iowa
Maryland Reporter	Annapolis, Maryland
MinnPost	Minneapolis, Minnesota
Montana Free Press	Helena, Montana
New England Center for Investigative Reporting	Boston, Massachusetts
New Haven Independent	New Haven, Connecticut
New Mexico In Depth	Albuquerque, New Mexico
NJ Spotlight	Newark, New Jersey
PA Post	Harrisburg, Pennsylvania
ProPublica	New York, New York
Rochester Beacon	Rochester, New York
San Jose Spotlight	San Jose, California
Seattle Globalist	Seattle, Washington
Sopris Sun	Carbondale, Colorado
St. Louis Public Radio (St. Louis Beacon)	St. Louis, Missouri
Texas Tribune	Austin, Texas
Voice of San Diego	San Diego, California

I also conducted field observations at two different nonprofits; the time spent would not qualify as ethnographic in nature, but did consist of multiple site visits in each instance. This data is augmented with interviews with other figures affecting nonprofit news work. In 2018, I conducted in-depth interviews with seven employees of five different funding organizations, decision-makers from journalism donors such as The Knight Foundation or the Democracy Fund. I also, in 2018, conducted shorter interviews with seven different companies that advertise on digitally native news nonprofit websites. I recruited these participants through emails. In all cases throughout this manuscript, the names of people and organizations have been anonymized to protect the identity of the source. Also, of note, this work couldn't be completed without the knowledge gained from the amazing work of other scholars studying nonprofit journalism and various funding models.

Notes

1 See Lewis and Cushion, "The thirst to be first," 306.
2 See Gans, *Deciding what's news*, or Tuchman, *Making news*.
3 See Saltzis, "Breaking news online."
4 See Nee, "Creative destruction."
5 See Gans, *Deciding what's news*, Tuchman, *Making news*, or Fishman, *Manufacturing the news*.
6 See Groves and Brown, "Stopping the presses."
7 See Nee, "Social responsibility theory and the digital nonprofits."
8 See Ferrucci, "Public journalism no more."
9 This statistic is courtesy of the Institute for Nonprofit News.
10 See Konieczna, *Journalism without profit*.
11 See Birnbauer, *The rise of nonprofit investigative journalism in the United States*.
12 For a thorough reading on public media, see Engelman, *Public radio and television in America*, and McChesney and Nichols, *The death and life of American journalism.*
13 For more on funding models, see Kaye and Quinn, *Funding journalism in the digital age*, or Larson, "Live publishing."
14 Both Ferrucci, "Follow the leader," and Kennedy, *The wired city* expand upon the founding of these organizations.
15 See Downie and Schudson, "The reconstruction of American journalism."
16 See Shoemaker and Reese, *Mediating the message in twenty-first century*, 1.
17 I do not examine the social system level in this work. This decision was primarily made because all organizations studied operate in the United States and therefore social system, or cultural, influences do not differ from other models of journalism in the United States.
18 Shoemaker and Reese's *Mediating the message in the twenty-first century* can provide a complete encapsulation of the model.
19 See Reese, "Understanding the global journalist," 174.
20 See Reese and Shoemaker, "A media sociology for the networked public sphere," 396.
21 See Vos and Heinderyckx, *Gatekeeping in transition*.
22 See Reese, *Understanding the global journalist*, 174.
23 For more on studies about how content from nonprofits differs from content produced by legacy media, see Ferrucci, *Murder incorporated*, and Ferrucci, "Primary differences."
24 I conducted an ethnography at the then *St. Louis Beacon* (currently *St. Louis Public Radio*) for my dissertation in 2013. I more recently, with the help of Colorado-Boulder Journalism Studies Ph.D. student Kathleen I. Alaimo, for a soon-to-be-published study in *Journalism*, did a case study of the *Sopris Sun*. In both of these cases, anonymity was not granted. However, for consistency in this book, I made all sources anonymous.
25 This list can be found here: https://inn.org/members/.

2　The journalists at nonprofits

In 2018, a 24-year-old journalist at a digitally native news nonprofit in the Midwest recalled an incident from her first six months on the job. After two internships at larger traditional daily newspapers and one at a nationally renowned digital organization, this reporter started at this nonprofit just short of two months after graduating from college. This would mark the first time she earned a paycheck to do journalism, a traditional marker of professional status within the industry.[1]

While in college, she volunteered at a well-known advocacy nonprofit, but quit her position after less than three months. "I came to realize," she said, "how (this organization) manipulated evidence and used it to recruit other people like me. (They) still do this. They try to mobilize millennials but the mission is unjust or even wrong." When she arrived at her first journalism job, her prior employer became part of the news after a candidate mentioned it in a presidential debate. This led the reporter to pitch a story about the organization. "I wanted to expose what I thought was hypocrisy and unethical behavior." Her editor found the pitch interesting and, six months in, the reporter believed she had her first big story. "I was going to tell everyone what I knew and it was going to make a difference," she recalled.

It didn't turn out that way, though.

After working on the story for roughly a month, the reporter could not corroborate much of what she thought she knew. The more she talked to sources at the advocacy organization and people who previously worked or volunteered there, the more she questioned her story. "I texted (my editor) because I wanted to change the story. He told me to do whatever I wanted." So the reporter returned to her sources, determined to find something newsworthy. After another week trying to uncover corruption, the reporter finally abandoned the story and instead wrote what essentially turned into an editorial about her experience. Looking back, she said, she wished she just dropped the story completely. "I was 20 when I worked (there)," she said roughly four years later. "I truly believed in that story at the time, but now I wonder if I was too idealistic and not completely processing how a large place operated." She now feels bad for writing the editorial because she "might have written things that accurately describe my truth, but not what typically happens there. Really, I was a small, small piece of a large operation and, back then, I thought I understood more than a I did." She said she now regrets giving her audience what could potentially be tainted information. "I'm glad (my editor) had faith in me to write something, but I shouldn't have done it. I could have hurt (that advocacy organization) and (my news organization)."

Implicit in that anecdote is the extent to which individual-level influences can impact news production processes at nonprofits. In works of media sociology, the manner in which individuals affect news decisions is quite well researched.[2] Journalists, in the course of news production processes, make hundreds of decisions due to numerous personal characteristics that provide individuals agency "even as they operate within larger constraints."[3] Some of the first studies examining news production squarely and singularly researched individual influence on news. For example, the classic *Mr. Gates* study by David Manning White illustrated how one wire editor's personal values and ideology impacted what appeared in a newspaper's wire copy section on a daily basis.[4] In the anecdote above, one could convincingly argue that individual-level influences such as age, experience, ideology, role conception and values highly impacted how the reporter covered that story. Overall, that anecdote specifically illustrates how this type of influence impacts newswork at nonprofits across the United States. This chapter outlines some specific influences that, according to the interviews conducted for this book, affect news production at news nonprofits generally. By illustrating how these specific influences affect news-production practices at nonprofits, this chapter demonstrates the relationship between the people working within journalism and the way that journalism is actually produced.

Age

The journalists interviewed for this book described the news nonprofit ecosystem as one filled with journalists on two extreme sides of an age continuum. Longtime, veteran journalists are the ones who often start nonprofit news organizations in the United States. In fact, many of the longest-running news nonprofits came into existence after older journalists retired or took relatively lucrative buyouts from legacy media.[5] Once they established a new nonprofit, they would then tend to hire either other veterans they worked with or recent college graduates who could be paid less.[6] This leaves a news organization without a middle-aged group, with just a group of journalists close to retirement and a group recently out of college. Some interviewees talked explicitly about this odd age range. One 25-year-old reporter said he noticed this right away.

> When I started at (my organization), almost immediately some of the other younger guys asked me to go get drinks. I'm talking about the first day. I quickly realized this was frequent. We have a lot of us who are young and not married or have kids and want to do the work and have fun. Everyone else, I think, mostly have kids, but those kids are sometimes older than us younger guys. We get treated like kids a lot. It doesn't happen in a bad or mean-spirited way, but I think the senior people here aren't used to dealing with twentysomethings in a co-worker capacity, you know?

That reporter is talking about extreme age difference in his newsroom by relating how the older journalists treat the younger ones, but this age difference remains even after nonprofits exist for some years. One older journalist with hiring power who's old enough to retire explained the difficulties of keeping younger journalists more than a couple years. "We've had maybe two people who came here young and stayed more than two or three years," he said. "I think we get them, make them better journalists and then can't pay them enough to stay. They end up getting a better journalism job or doing something else." Essentially, this age range continuously exists because younger reporters move on or older reporters retire, and both groups tend to be replaced by younger journalists. If an older editor retires, they are often replaced by another older journalist close to retirement. "In my nine years here," said one older editor, "we have hired one person over the age of 30 and under the age of 60. A lot of hires have come to us too." While no other interviewee said something so explicitly, this sentiment was echoed numerous times.

Beyond turnover, age also impacts performance. This chapter opened with an anecdote about a younger journalist pursuing a story and eventually publishing a critical opinion column about a nonprofit advocacy organization. Now, even that journalist acknowledges her column could have been a mistake. By employing so many younger journalists, nonprofit news organizations are more apt to make small or large mistakes. This puts a greater responsibility on older journalists to remain highly critical when editing copy. One editor jested about this:

> I was buying new business cards a year or two ago and I looked through the options at home. I joked to my husband that the card

should say "politics editor" and "journalism professor." Obviously, you know I don't work at a college, but I feel like I do since a lot of my time is spent teaching some of our really young reporters or the interns we get from (a local university).

Not only older journalists expressed this sentiment. Multiple younger journalists interviewed positively remarked on the way they learned from older journalists in the newsroom. One talked about how he "looks up to (his older coworkers)" and believes he would be "ignorant if (he) didn't try to absorb as much as (he) can from them."

The final way that age influences news construction in a nonprofit newsroom comes from the way it helps to shape the adoption of technology. The vast majority of nonprofits in this country are online only,[7] and thus label themselves as digital journalism.[8] However, participants from both age ranges noted that actual digital journalism only comes from younger reporters. Older reporters "do text," said one younger reporter. "That's it," he said, adding, "we do multimedia, all of it." This is not surprising since many newsrooms hire younger journalists because of their technology skills;[9] however, this dichotomy was mentioned numerous times. Older journalists generally acknowledged what the younger ones brought to the organization. One said,

> We have this one guy who can do anything. He helped me create an interactive visual for a story that I could never (have) even imagined. To be honest, it was better than my story itself. He's not typical since I've never met anyone that good, but our fresher-faced reporters can all do some great things with video. Everything on our site that's video is done by them.

Some of the younger journalists believe that these skills in technology provide a way to equalize what each age group brings to the specific organization. Multiple participants mentioned that while they might not know as much about journalism as a whole, their organization needs technology to thrive. "Can you imagine if, in 2017, we only put words and images on our site?" asked one younger journalist. He continued by essentially arguing that twenty-first-century journalism needs to be multimedia and, especially, video-heavy because "that's how people do news now." Another younger journalist talked about trying to teach older journalists how use their phones to gather video for a story. She said, in one particular instance, she had planned to follow-up by teaching someone how to edit video after they understood how to gather video. "I gave up after I saw the video (he) took at the speech he was covering. I thought it was a lost cause." This sentiment came up so often that it is clear that age impacts the media form used to tell stories at nonprofits.

Experience

While experience and age would seemingly impact news production in broadly the same way, that is not entirely true. According to the data collected, there were some key differences. This became especially evident when an organization hired a younger person without, for example, an internship or a journalism degree. One veteran journalist remarked on this by explaining

> I was an English major at university. I never put too much weight into journalism degrees. But we've hired some history or similar majors recently. They come in with no experience at all or maybe they did this or that at the school newspaper. They're lost. They are more in need of all types of guidance than the 22 or 23 year old with some professional experience or schooling in the area.

Experience, according to interviewees, impacts numerous areas of news production, specifically how journalists perceive the norms of the industry, how they define success, and the type of sources they utilize.

Norms. The less experience a journalist has, the less likely s/he is to not only follow traditional journalism norms, but to even think of those behaviors positively.[10] For example, one journalist with less than two years of experience said,

> Everybody at [my organization] who's been here for any real amount of time talks about certain standards like they came down from god. My teachers [in college] did too. I think they do this not because they believe this is the right way to journalize, but because it gives them power.[11]

That quote illustrates how journalists with less professional experience can sometimes feel threatened by what they perceive as unneeded rules. A journalist with more than two decades professional experience echoed these comments, but from the other side of it. He said, "Some of these new kids, they don't want to do journalism and only want to tell what they think are cool stories." That interviewee went on to say that some less-experienced journalists, ones not steeped in norms, believe that getting a story is all that matters and the process by which the reporting happens is unimportant. When talking about norms, most participants implicitly discussed ethics or verification. For example, when talking about a less experienced journalist that was let go from her organization, one interviewee said,

> I don't think he ever checked facts. I mean that. He worked here for nine months, right out of school, and didn't know the first thing about how to be a journalist. He would use Wikipedia or Google something and put it in. Or he would take a source's word for everything. I see this a lot with people who haven't been burned before. They believe everything. Once they've done this long enough and get burnt, everything becomes different.

But while ethics and verification came up often in connection with experience, how journalists engaged with the audience was also discussed. Participants noted that the more experience a journalist accrues, the more negatively they view using social media for engagement.[12] Regardless of age, the journalists said, more experience meant journalists would use social media less and less to engage with the audience during news production. "I don't mean sources overall," said one journalist, "but Facebook. You use it for a while and you realize it's a sham. It doesn't work for getting people involved. But when they first get here, I believe they're gung ho." When talking to one interviewee who, at the time, had about two months' professional experience, this sentiment became clear. He said,

> The aspect of (this organization) I'm most disappointed with is how non-existent social media networks are in the newsroom. Can't journalism be better if it's reaching more people? Those networks can help do that. When I think about it, they're a real untapped resource and hope I can convince some people of that.

Success. Newsroom experience impacted how journalists define success. In a general way, the more experience a journalist accrued, the more likely they were to see success in terms of the organization or the public, while less-experienced journalists often viewed success as a personal gain. For example, when discussing how they thought of success, many journalists with more experience explicitly talked about making an impact on policy or publishing a story that helps the public. For example, one journalist with experience said that the best they ever felt as a journalist came when publishing a story that helped to convince a city to provide more funding for the homeless. Less experienced journalists oftentimes discussed success more specifically in terms of personal accomplishments. In one such case, a less-experienced journalist explicitly discussed the ability to publish a "viral" story as success. He said,

> I did a piece about three months ago that we published to our main Twitter account. After about two hours, I went and looked at the post. I was really just curious. I want to say it had been retweeted like 400 times. That's so much more than ever before. I did some more checking and others (tweeted about the story) without actually retweeting (the link) too. It was a big deal. I definitely think the other people here took note.

When discussing that viral story, the reporter never mentioned what the story was about or how it had any impact beyond the retweets. This was relatively common overall when examining the difference in how experience impacts how journalists perceive success. Of course, if journalists are perceiving success in such a different manner, this could very easily be affecting how they choose stories or even how they frame them.

Sources. Experience also impacts how journalists choose sources. According to the data, the journalists with more experience favored more expert sources, while less-experienced journalists tended to include more "regular people" in their stories. This could happen for a variety of reasons. First, the more experience a journalist accrues, the more chances they have to cultivate expert sources. For example, one experienced journalist said he felt bad for less-experienced journalists because they arrived at the job "without a digital Rolodex of the important people here." A less experienced journalist echoed these thoughts when she talked about the hardest part of starting her job. "I didn't know anyone," she said. "If a story happened and I needed a quote, I would ask a coworker who to call when I needed someone who would know about the topic." Therefore, because of their lack of a "digital Rolodex," many less-experienced journalists compensate by incorporating more regular people into stories. Some perceive they do this out of necessity. One said, "If I'm struggling with sources, a man-on-the-street vibe is the thing to do." Others, though, reasoned that this was the way to do journalism properly. One less-experienced journalist said,

> I think the community has a lot of important shit to say. They know better than you and me what's important. A lot of people I work with, they always talk to the people we should criticizing and that makes for a situation where only one type of voice is heard. We need to hear the everyman's voice. I try to help with that.

Ideology

While journalists are often derisively considered part of the "liberal media," at nonprofits, there is more than likely some truth to the idea that journalists tend to lean left. Journalists self-select into their profession, so there are many commonalities within the profession.[13] At nonprofits, this leads to more liberal journalists. As one journalist noted,

> I don't think it's some great eureka moment to say most journalists are Democrats or even more liberal than that. But I would say (this organization) is even less diverse. At other places I've worked, we've always had some fiscal conservatives or something close to that. We rarely had social conservatives, but I'm getting away from my point. Here, we're all the same in terms of how we think about the world. That means we're pretty cohesive as a whole.

The liberal nature of most of these newsrooms can come through in how they select stories. Numerous journalists interviewed talked explicitly about uncovering conservative corruption or debunking, what one person called, "Republican gobble-de-gook." It's important to note that literally nobody equated these ideas with unethical behavior or doing anything that would amount to providing the public with untrue information. However, numerous journalists simply identified, for example, publicizing the "lies of the right" as an important goal, especially in the late 2010s. As one journalist explained,

> Look at the times we live in. Half of our country doesn't believe in climate change because we have a political party that can lie with impunity since the people they're talking to are either naïve or intentionally ignorant or dumb. That's true. If I want to really help people, I need to make sure I call out these lies and tell our people coming to the website why this is a lie, who said it and what is the truth. That's my job right now. We have a lot of liars running our country, yes, but they're also in my backyard here in (the state I work in).

The idea that conservatives are more likely to spread disinformation is commonplace in nonprofit newsrooms. One journalist at a nonprofit in a traditionally conservative state relayed how this belief got him in trouble once. "I absolutely fact-check Republicans harder," said the journalist. "When I covered a gubernatorial debate during the last cycle, I did that hard (to one candidate) and not (the Democrat). In that case, the Democrat was a bigger liar and my fact-checks didn't show that." The reporter went on to say that his news organization rightfully received a significant amount of criticism for pointing out all of the Republican candidate's lies, but only selectively doing the same with the Democrat candidate. A different interviewee talked about a very similar situation, one that also resulted in some criticism for his organization. He said he got a tip from a trusted source about a conservative politician. The tip turned out to be false, but the reporter believed it wholeheartedly due to his opinion of conservatives. This led to trying to verify the tip for days and, when he could not, publishing the tip with a blind quote from the source. "I was wrong and that came out pretty soon. My source played me, I think."

Political ideology also affects how journalists at nonprofits seek out story topics. Journalists often talked about pursuing stories based on their political beliefs. Again, no interviewee ever admitted to letting their ideology affect the content of a particular story, but the data suggest ideology affected the topic. For example, many journalists openly discussed how they believed climate change was one of the most important topics impacting the country. Participants, one with a background in covering the environment and another without such a background, admitted to looking for stories to write about climate change. One explained,

> Climate change will kill us soon. People need to know. If I can find some angle that lets me write about global warming, I take it. It's a civic duty. I look for a particular type of story. I want graphic things. I think people need to understand climate issues viscerally.

In another instance, a reporter provided an anecdote about how Planned Parenthood was "under assault" in his state. He mentioned that two clinics closed in the year before the interview. This led to a story.

> Someone else covered the closures. That wasn't me. But the whole rhetoric about Planned makes me mad. You know, it's stupid in, like, a harmful way. I wanted to explain all the good things Planned does for a community. I went out and just hung out in the parking lot of one of the (clinics) left and interviewed everyone. The story was about how low-income people, women really, needed Planned for essential needs. The story never once, like, used the word abortion. I made that choice because of the rhetoric that always connected Planned Parenthood to abortion, only abortion.

Journalists often also chose less investigative pieces based on ideology. Numerous journalists interviewed discussed the relative autonomy they held in terms of choosing stories. This impacted, for example, which subjects reporters profiled. Two journalists at different organizations admitted that if you added up profiles their organizations published on politicians, one would find far more liberal subjects than conservative subjects. One explained this happened because of untruths. "I'd like more puff pieces or something about Republicans," he said, "but if everything they say is a lie, I can't, you know, write the story." Besides personality profiles, the same process for determining organizations to profile or cover also occurred. One journalist explained, "I cover a city with a major conservative thinktank. They hold events pretty regularly. We cover some of those, but a lot of times what they're pushing is so odious, I just can't."

Overall, due to the overwhelming liberalness of the journalists at nonprofits, the news production processes can be impacted. The type of stories covered and topics chosen can be influenced by how the journalist views the subject or how they perceive the topic, which is often shaped by their political ideology.

Values

In his landmark work of media sociology *Deciding what's news*,[14] Hebert Gans identified some of the personal values of journalists that end up assisting in the shaping of news. For example, Gans noted that many journalists adhere to a set of social values prevalent in the United States such as small-town pastoralism or the idea of responsible capitalism. Out of the eight values that Gans uncovered, though, the journalists interviewed for this book only mentioned one: Altruistic democracy. This value implicitly came up in almost every single interview with journalists at nonprofits. This value "represents politics and government as operating in the public interest."[15]

The most general impact of this adherence to the social value of altruistic democracy comes in the form of overall journalistic content. While most legacy newsrooms, particularly the ones that digitally native news nonprofit founders worked at previously, cover general news, the majority of the nonprofit organizations examined focus almost exclusively one or two topics. For example, many of the organizations spend roughly 20 percent of their resources on coverage of cultural issues and the rest on political coverage. Very few organizations ever published pieces on sports or entertainment, two very prevalent topics at traditional newspapers. The frequency with which these organizations cover politics comes from a sincere belief by leadership that politics are the absolute most important topic to understand in a democracy. One editor and co-founder of a nonprofit explicitly said she helped start her organization due to what her last organization covered:

We had more reporters, by far, at spring training baseball games fawning over (the home team) than we did at city hall or the state house. I couldn't take it much longer. How are people supposed to vote on their own behalf if they barely know anything happening? That's our job as journalists, isn't it?

Inherent in that statement is the idea that in a democracy, information about our government is power. Citizens, implied many interviewees, cannot act in their own best interests if they do not understand how government is operating.

For Gans, by adhering to this social value, journalists often tended to write more negative stories. This hypothesis bore out in terms of the perceptions of the journalists I interviewed. When discussing how they covered government and politics, they often explicitly discussed looking for abuses of power. To strengthen democracy, they argued, journalists always needed to be on the lookout for corruption. One journalist discussed this specifically:

> My job, first and foremost, is to be looking for those taking advantage of the public trust. Politicians or even government employees take an oath, sometimes literally but most of the time figuratively, to help people. We, as a country, are getting away from that, dude. Politicians don't always even pretend to care about us, the people, anymore.

The journalists believe that uncovering this type of story not only strengthens democracy, but assists in the optimal running of government. They often spoke about how government operates "in the shadows" and "putting a spotlight" on those operations can only be good for society. If government is working properly, it does not need attention. A journalist said this specifically:

> I don't understand why anybody would think we need more good news. I had an editor somewhere say that a lot. By definition, good news isn't news. That might be harsh, or just sound harsh, and obviously I think journalists ought to cover good things sometimes. Bad news, a term I hate, is what matters most. When a politician does literally anything bad, it matters more than anything good to people. I really believe that.

While generally the journalists discussed negative stories as the optimal manner they could manifest altruistic democracy, the data illustrated two very specific types of stories are most commonly looked at as part of this social value. First, the vast majority of the journalists identified stories about tax dollars as an essential element of their organization's coverage. They perceived these stories as essential to the public interest. "If people don't know where their money goes," said one journalist, "how can they make any decision?" This sentiment was echoed consistently. One journalist relayed an anecdote that neatly sums up this belief.

> What I consider the important story of my career really had to do with a cigarette tax. The state heavily taxes tobacco compared to other similar states. The money went to a handful of projects, but people were told the highest percentage would go to schools. I don't even remember why I started work on the story. Really right after I started, I began to realize the most money was not going to education. I published the story. Things changed after that. The story made a real difference.

Other journalists discussed this topic in a more overall sense, meaning not about stories they actually published, but as one of the ways they covered politics. "Asking candidates what they'll do with tax monies," said one interviewee, "can produce good stories. But it can also help the public make strongly educated choices. Where the money goes is something we should know."

The other type of stories specifically identified that could be connected to altruistic democracy are stories about how politics work. "Those pieces are sort of inside baseball," said one journalist, explaining that many members of the public could understand specific issues, but they do not understand how those issues get voted on, for example. A different journalist explicitly mentioned campaign ads as a good example of why stories like this are needed. He said,

> You know those TV ads during elections that mention how so and so voted against this thing you should never vote against? The ads usually mention this in like words spoken and also words on the screen? Yeah, well, a lot of people don't know that politicians will sometimes add things to amendments or bills just as gotcha. Here in (this state), we had what was basically you can't kill a baby after it's born thrown in to some inoffensive bill that everyone knew would be voted down. Then commercial after commercial said so and so voted against a bill that would have made it illegal to kill a baby after it's born. I wrote a story explaining how that all went down.

Other journalists interviewed discussed similar stories, ones meant to teach the general public about how government operates. If people understand how government operates and politicians conduct business, they will be less likely to believe the kind of advertisements described above. "Stories like the one I described," said a journalist, "I consider those more about civic literacy than anything else."

Identity

To better understand how journalists do their jobs, it is important to account for their professional identity. Professional identity is just one part of a person's overall identity, which is made up of a number of official or unofficial affiliations in social groups.[16] For journalists, a large portion of their overall identity comes in the form of their professional identity. This is perhaps best illustrated by a recent study that found even when journalists leave the profession, they still consider themselves journalists and that the occupation plays an outsized role in their overall identity.[17] In the past, professional identity was often seen as something stable, something that journalists could conceive without worrying what it meant to themselves and others.[18] Because the very concept of journalist is in a state of flux, some now consider journalistic professional identity "liquid," meaning something that is constantly able to change.[19] This is why, when studying identity, it is vital to understand "how journalists identify themselves can also be understood in terms of how they conceive of the social role of journalism."[20]

Numerous scholars have studied role conception, but nonprofit journalists are both similar and different in terms of how they conceive their jobs as journalists.[21] Journalists at nonprofits fundamentally identify two traditional roles: The watchdog and the disseminator, as fundamental to their jobs. They also noted a new role, the community advocate, which suggests their organization type can impact role.[22] It's important to remember, though, that while the journalists interviewed talked about these roles as ones they conceive for themselves, ones that make up a significant portion of their identity, this does not mean they enact these roles.[23]

Watchdog. Unsurprisingly since journalists held the social value of altruistic democracy strongly, the most common role identified by interviewees was the watchdog. Each and every interviewee, at some point during the interview, explicitly talked about the need to be a check on power. They discussed the role as something essential to a democracy. One said,

> Who is going to make sure our leaders stay in line? Who is going to make sure the caucus runs on the up and up? The answer has to be journalism. Think about it: No other institution is set up to curtail

abuses of power. Without us, what would politicians fear? They could do what they want.

This sentiment came up consistently. Another journalist noted that "the press is all that stands between what we have now and an aristocracy." She basically meant that without the press, people in power would stay in power and become leaders who were not elected in a fair system. The need for the watchdog role implicitly coincides with that last statement; journalists believe that governments and, specifically, powerful people are corrupt or prone to corruption. One interviewee brought up ancient history to make his point:

> Go back in time and tell me when unfettered power didn't lead to abuses. It always does. People are always going to do the wrong thing so they can keep what they have. All governments eventually fail because they do so many awful things, people rebel and a coup happens. Journalists make sure none of that happens because we take note of the symptoms, the ones that could lead to bad consequences, and we inform. That's a big check on people.

Another interviewee did not fault politicians or prominent figures, instead the reporter just acknowledged that power corrupts.

> All senators or politicians aren't bad. That's not what I'm saying. It's the position that's bad. Look at Obama. I don't think he's crooked or anything, and that's not what I'm talking about. But he took office under a cloud of optimism and was going to make a difference. Soon he fell in with all the usual suspects spouting pseudo liberal things while ultimately siding with the bankers. That's what happens when these guys – and they're almost always men – become prominent politicians. I have this idea that a big part of my job is to call this out.

Yet while nonprofit journalists perceive the watchdog role in relation to, predominantly, politicians, they also occasionally talked about the role concerning businesses in their respective areas. In fact, some of the interviewees went as far as calling businesses "the new government," or something similar. They see their role as not only monitoring politicians, but keeping track of how major businesses treat employees, contribute to government, pay taxes and regulate themselves. "Only in the last 15 or so years, I think," said one journalist, "have we come to understand the way big companies control just about everything." That particular journalist noted that corporations spend vast quantities of money on lobbying the government to enact policies that will be economically positive for them. However, these policies could be obviously detrimental to the public. These corporations also attempt to navigate around paying taxes, said one journalist, and this, she noted, connects to the aforementioned focus on publishing material concerning taxes. One journalist summed up the need to cover businesses:

> The fat cats, guy. They are shady a lot of times. Think about the intrigue surrounding major corporations or conglomerates. You typically have unethical dealings happening with executives, sometimes, lately, sexual harassment or worse. You have billion dollar companies paying less tax than me. You have employees getting paid shit compared to what the companies make. You have an emphasis on stock prices above all else. And these places control local economies a lot of times, so the government has to keep them happy or unemployment happens and elected officials lose their jobs. The stories are totally endless when thinking about how to cover this stuff.

When discussing the watchdog role, nonprofit journalists often explicitly or implicitly argued it was essential for democracy and the main role of journalism. The journalists mentioned multiple other role conceptions, but when discussing the watchdog role, the implication almost could be interpreted as without the particular role, an organization was not practicing journalism. Multiple times interviewees called journalism the "fourth estate" and noted that it is ultimately necessary if we truly covet democracy. One journalist said,

> I don't know if any of us could have ever predicted this type of polarization all over us. We used to have three distinct branches of government federally. We still do, sort of, at the state level. Federally, though, I don't think so. Everyone just toes the party line and very few, close to nada, stand up for the right thing. Washington and Jefferson and that group envisioned checks and balances. The Supreme Court is not checking or balancing Trump. The House and Senate aren't checking or balancing Trump. Journalists are. In the last year and change, it's us. What would have happened if not for us?

Disseminator. The other traditional journalism role conception mentioned often by the interviewees was the disseminator role. This role is conceptualized as journalists delivering information to the public, and many nonprofit journalists discursively create their professional identities with this role prevalent. The journalists consistently talked about "getting information to people" or "telling everyone what's going on" as a main component of their jobs. One interviewee describes his job at a nonprofit as, "Basically, I keep people in the loop." The journalists believe that a main function of journalism is to disseminate information to a mass audience; that audience is determined by the reach of the news organization. Another interviewee essentially equated journalism with more important entertainment, arguing "HBO" provides people with compelling films and television shows for their enjoyment, while "news" provides people with compelling information for their "knowledge and entertainment." The journalists see themselves as professionals out in the field, working toward uncovering vital information that they will then shape and frame to fit the audience. Finally, they then send this journalism to the audience through a specific media channel. Essentially, for this role at nonprofits, the idea is going out and getting news and then publishing it in some way.

Many nonprofit journalists hold the disseminator role in high regard and import because, they believe, if their organization does not enact this role, the public will suffer. They consistently noted that they believe their organization disseminates information to the public because others do not. One editor and co-founder said,

> What (my organization) does best is obvious, I think. We get people the news they need. If you look around this city, watch the TV broadcasts or read (the main newspaper), you'll see a lot of crap and Associated Press copy. Those outlets we compete with aren't truly covering the city. There is a void that we fill. If we didn't, people would be yearning for more. That's why we did (this organization).

This sentiment was expressed in numerous ways. Many, like the above quotation, openly questioned how competitors in legacy media covered their communities. Some interviewees called legacy media "shit" or "just short of rubbish" or, more gently, "trying hard to do their best with hedge funds gutting them to the core." Regardless of how they were categorized, nonprofit journalists do not believe legacy media remain a quality disseminator. They believe that is why nonprofit organizations continue multiplying across the country. "The future of media is public," said one journalist, adding,

> These companies will continue sucking the blood out of daily newspapers. When I first started at (a major metropolitan newspaper), our crew of the desk had more people than the entire news department there now. That's not an exaggeration. If you do not count the sports department, we had more city desk journalists then than they have journalists now.

The interviewees believe that nonprofits would not have thrived, for example, in the twentieth century because the audience received enough quality information from legacy media; they did not need another outlet. But, now, as one journalist said, "people desire news," and legacy media is not quenching that desire.

The final way that nonprofit journalists enacted the disseminator role intersected with technology. The journalists believe that part of their professional role concerns "reaching people where they are," as described by one journalist. To these interviewees, being a disseminator meant getting information to the public in the most optimal manner. Many of these not only felt, for example, that legacy media did not cover the news very well, but, also, when they did, it failed to reach much of an audience. One journalist explained,

> If you're primarily publishing news in a newspaper or on an awful website, who's reading it? I would say that, probably, an older demographic is. That group of people is informed though. But I want to make sure everyone can read my stuff. To me, that means making sure we publish our stories across channels.

What this journalist believes is that if news is only disseminated via traditional media, a large segment of the population will not receive it. Likeminded journalists often connected social media to this role. They believe that to reach a large audience, journalism must be nimble and literate with social media since that is where a significant portion of the audience receives news. They believe in thinking about how a story will be disseminated during the reporting process. For example, one journalist explained,

> When I start a story, I'm all for brainstorming how I would want to see it. That matters. I think we need to tell stories differently depending on their subject matter. I try to think, what would this look like in print or on video or as a link and graphic on (Facebook)? I don't have proof, but I'm thinking when I do that, it's easier for me and my editors to tailor the piece to more than one platform.

The journalist went on to say that if a story is disseminated over multiple platforms, a larger audience will see it and, potentially consume it. This makes for more successful dissemination, which, in turn, means a journalist believes they are doing a better job accomplishing their role as a disseminator.

Community advocate. Prior research into role conceptions and journalism identified the role of "populist mobilizer" after the industry began implementing practices from movements such as public journalism. This role mainly detailed how journalists aimed to engage the community and build community through reporting.[24] For nonprofit journalists, the role of community advocate is similar, but ultimately there are nuanced differences. These journalists believe they are part of the community, not just someone mobilizing the community. "When I'm fighting for them," said one journalist, "I'm fighting for myself, of course." They believe their position as a journalist is almost similar to an elected official voted into office to carry out the public's wishes. A journalist explained this as,

> I'm someone who should only be doing what my community tells me to do. I need to be in constant contact, going back and forth to make sure what I'm doing best represents them. That's the nature of this job. I work for them. Too many journalists see it the opposite way and that's what makes news not connect to people.

For these journalists, the need to effectively tend to the public's wishes is their role as a journalist. This can overlap with other roles such as the watchdog, but ultimately this is the main role of a journalist, according to these interviewees. Everything else is secondary.

One of the main goals of the community advocate role is to bring the community together. The journalists who conceive this professional role believe that enacting it properly will lead to a more unified public. For example, one journalist called himself a "unifier" who aims to "get past differences and make everything kumbaya." Another journalist said she hopes that in her role as a journalist, she's helping to "remove barriers between people." She explained this as,

> There's so much out there at the moment forcing people apart. It's literally what some people want. If we the public can't get along, then we can't accomplish anything. There will always be things that some disagree on, you know? The thing is most things we should agree on, but limited or biased information keeps us apart. I want to fix that issue.

These journalists think providing quality information to people should be in the pursuit of bringing a community together. This can happen if the journalism produced is of importance to the people, said many journalists. They believe intimately that if the public understands something, in most cases, they will all come to the same "rational" conclusion and, in the process, see there are "more things bringing us together than keeping us apart." A main reason that so much division occurs throughout the country, on both a micro and macro level, says these journalists, is because of a lack of quality information. "If we can fix" this lack of unbiased information, "then we can get back to disagreeing on things where there is no common ground like abortion and not on silliness like climate change."

Another way that this community advocate role can be enacted is by always taking the community's side. This idea again overlaps with the watchdog role in that both revolve around holding people accountable. This part of the community advocate role, though, dismisses the concept of objectivity and openly takes on a bias in favor of the community. One journalist said,

> I believe my role as a journalist is to be the eyes and ears and loud voice of the people. I'm their representative and I'm better at it than fucking crooked politicians. I try to make their lives better.[25]

The implicit message in that quote conveys that a community advocate takes on the persona of the community and does so in a very public and up-front manner. It is not enough to simply watchdog people in power, a journalist must always aim to make the public's "lives better" and represent them in the act of journalism. For these journalists, the news is not about just disseminating what the industry considers "newsworthy," it's about articulating the public's wants and needs. The manner in which this must be accomplished is whatever way results in the public receiving what it wants. One journalist said,

> I'm with the people. I'm on that side. If you're not a regular person then we're not on the same team. I really get behind that feeling. Journalists, at least I think, get caught up in the idea of not taking sides and being balanced or whatever synonym you want to use. When did that start? I was always told we're doing things for the public. So then we can't be balanced, right? We need to be for them. Full stop.

For nonprofit journalists, these three role conceptions – the disseminator, the watchdog and the community advocate – represent how they construct their identities. While these include two traditional roles, the presence of the community advocate illustrates how the very idea of journalistic professional identity is slightly shifting, or "liquid," and this could especially be the case at nonprofits, which were predominantly started as a response to what founders perceived as a lack of quality – and quality can mean many things – at local legacy organizations.

This chapter does not identity any new individual-level influences shaping journalism at digitally native news nonprofits. There are novel demographics listed here that could lead to a robust survey that researchers have not already conducted with journalism practitioners. But, as will be the case throughout this book, the makeup of these individual-level variables and the way they impose their influence absolutely do differ at nonprofits in a way that should be focused on in future research. For example, the nuanced differences in the way journalists at nonprofits conceive their professional roles or construct their identities significantly impact news production.

Notes

1 For a more thorough explanation of how organizational backing usually impacts professional status, see Ferrucci and Vos, "Who's in, who's out," or Peters and Tandoc, "People who aren't really reporters at all."
2 See Shoemaker and Vos, *Gatekeeping theory.*
3 See Shoemaker and Reese, *Mediating the message*, 204.
4 See White, "The 'gate keeper.'"
5 See Ferrucci, "Follow the leader," or Kennedy, *The wired city.*
6 For a good example of how this happens, see Kennedy, *The wired city*, or Russell, "Silicon Valley and the new gatekeepers."
7 See Batsell, *Engaged journalism* or Konieczna, *Journalism without profit.*
8 See Carlson and Usher, "News startups as agents of innovation."
9 See Ferrucci, "We've lost the basics."
10 See Vos, "Journalists' endangered professional status" for an example of how professionalism, and thus norms, are changing.
11 This quote originally appeared in Ferrucci, "Are you experienced," 2424, a piece that examines that impact of experience on the industry as a whole.
12 For a more thorough discussion of this subject, see Belair-Gagon, "News on the fly."
13 See, for example, Weaver and Wilhoit, *The American journalist in the 1990s.*
14 See Gans, *Deciding what's news.*
15 See Shoemaker and Vos, *Gatekeeping theory*, 44.
16 See Kopytowska and Kalyango, *Why discourse matters.*
17 See Sherwood and O'Donnell, "Once a journalist, always a journalist?"
18 For a good understanding of how journalists conceived their identities in the recent past, see Deuze, "What is journalism?" and Deuze, "The professional identity of journalists in the context of convergence culture."
19 See Jaakkola, Hellman, Koljonen, and Väliverronen, "Liquid modern journalism with a difference."
20 See Vos and Ferrucci, "Who am I?," 870.
21 For the most thorough research on journalism and role conception, see the studies by Weaver and colleagues on journalists through the decades.
22 See Painter and Ferrucci, "Digital marketplace."
23 See Tandoc, Hellmueller and Vos, "Mind the gap."
24 See Weaver et al., *The American journalist in the 21st century.*
25 This quote originally appeared in Painter and Ferrucci, "Digital marketplace," 115.

3   The routines of newsmaking at nonprofits

After receiving a story assignment from an editor, a reporter at a digitally native news nonprofit on the East Coast begins doing some research on the subject. She knows about the topic, but describes her knowledge as "definitely not at the level needed to write a story." The reporter spent approximately three hours gathering information through previously written stories on the topic and by reading comments left on those stories by readers and journalists. The topic involved a controversial political bill passed by her local legislature. At most newsrooms, her next step would be to begin contacting a group of sources that would include politicians who voted on both sides and established activist organizations in favor of or against the bill.

"I try not to use expert sources," she explained. This means that instead of contacting people intimately involved in the bill, this reporter set out to understand the public's take on it. Her newsroom subscribes to an "engagement" product that fundamentally allows for her to search a database of what she calls "regular people I can use for sources." She explained why her newsroom uses this service:

> My editor believes that journalists use the same sources over and over again. Those people sometimes don't represent who we should represent. With (this product), I can find regular people who care about whatever topic I'm reporting on. It's not very different than Google. I just type in the topic and anybody who signed up and labeled themselves interested in that topic will come up in my search query. Then I start looking at them to kind of, maybe, decide who fits best with the story I'm telling. (The product) means I won't use the same sources for stories.

For this story specifically, the reporter was able to find someone whose child would be directly affected by the bill. "The parents didn't even know about the law change," said the reporter about her found source. She scheduled an interview and went over to the source's house. At the meeting, the reporter spent time explaining the potential new law. Before the interview, the reporter sent over research so the source could have some contextual information, but felt a thorough, in-person explanation seemed necessary.

When finished with the explanation, the interview began. The reporter really wanted to focus on how this bill could affect the source's child. This, the reporter thought, was the best way to tell the story. She explained,

> The mother gave me so much. So much. She went into detail about how each piece of the proposed law could affect (her son). Through her, I began to understand the implications of this political move in a way that my research or even base knowledge on the subject could never get to. She took the time to explain everything in detail. Then when I wrote the story up, it has to be half from that interview. This personal connection to the law is what makes the story come alive and, I think, helps the reader understand the real-life implications of something that might have seemed far away or just procedural.

After completing the interview with this source, the reporter then went and interviewed two distinct "expert" sources. Instead of questioning them about very specific elements of the bill, she instead told them both her source's story and asked them to comment on it. "I wanted (the sources) to speak plainly about how the things they do affect real people," she said. "I think forcing (one source) to defend his vote in the face of a prime example of the hurt the bill causes is the way we should approach stories like this."

The manner in which this reporter approached the story illustrates the power of communication routines on news production practices at nonprofit news organizations. This reporter's orientation to the audience and to expert sources, particularly, impacted how this story unfolded for the public. Her specific choices about the news values of a story and the bias inherent in how she told this particular story clearly influenced the news production process. When asked about it, the reporter admitted this particular routine was far from unique in her daily workday. In fact, numerous journalists interviewed relayed very similar processes, practices that cut across various nonprofit news organizations.

The communication routines level of analysis describes the "routine practices of communication work, rules – mostly unwritten – that give the media worker guidance."[1] When discussing communication routines, these are practices embedded within an organization, but, really, independent of any one particular newsroom; these are the journalistic practices that transcend newsrooms and "do not develop randomly" as they are prevalent across the industry.[2] Routines are essential to understanding how journalists, specifically, report on any potential story. In the anecdote above, any different decision, from starting with expert sources to wanting to obtain "both sides" of the story, would have greatly influenced the content eventually consumed by the public. To many scholars studying news production in the twentieth century, influences from communication routines impacted journalism practice more than anything else,[3] so that "journalism routines are a distinct explanatory factor of news content."[4] Broadly explained, the manners in which journalists do their jobs affects news production in a disproportionate way.

The interviewees for this book identified several routines-level factors that help shape their newswork. As noted in this chapter's opening anecdote, the journalist's orientation to the audience, orientation to sources and estimation of the concept of objectivity, all impact news. But, also, the way nonprofit journalists define and identity news values, the fact-checking processes embedded in journalistic practice, the journalists' adherence to the concept of iconoclasm, and the way ethical practices are incorporated into routines all impact news production processes at nonprofit news organizations.[5] Interviewees specifically mention or implied each of these seven distinct factors consistently in the data.

Orientation to sources

The ideas for news stories do not, primarily, come from the minds of journalists. In reality, "reporters typically gather news from official government proceedings, news releases, news conferences, and non-spontaneous events such as ceremonies and speeches."[6] How journalists engage with these different news sources helps explain their orientation to sources. For nonprofit journalists, the way they define an expert source and the way they utilize those expert sources is seemingly very intentional and impactful. The vast majority of the journalists interviewed described the need to branch out when considering expert sources. For example, one journalist explicitly mentioned that most news organizations limit their pool of congressmen and women to interview, but his newsroom attempts to talk to more than just the most quotable. A different journalist discussed how during a gubernatorial race, his nonprofit organization was the only one to cover third-party candidates or, during the primary, down-ballot candidates. He said this was important because if you don't cover lesser-known candidates, "you're helping to make sure they're opinions aren't heard."

When discussing one particular candidate during a gubernatorial primary, one journalist explained why he thought it important to cover a candidate not receiving any coverage elsewhere. He said,

> But I think that we wanted to have a more robust, comprehensive view of the race, and to do that, you had to include him in there somehow. I don't think you have to focus on him intently, but especially if there is a forum and all are there, all of them have views on things, something he said could be an issue or an insight that can come back later either at a future race or election.[7]

This sentiment came up numerous times in interviews with many journalists noting that the way they seek out sources sometimes revolves around interviewing and talking to experts usually ignored for some unknown reason.

Another way that journalists at nonprofits utilize expert sources in a potentially altered manner concerns the very definition of an expert source. "Most places look for well-known figures or organizations," explained one journalist, adding, "but I'm trying to find the people who really know about something but we wouldn't call an expert." When asked for an example, the journalist described covering a school board vote:

> The board voted on a measure that would change how certain subjects would be taught. If you look at (my competitors') coverage the next day, the sources were principally the school board, people at the meeting and in one case, a member of a school board that made a similar vote in the recent past. I don't think people care about why a school board member voted the way they did. I take that back; they care, but not as much as they care about why it all matters. My story sought the teachers this would have an impact on. I also interviewed two recently graduated students who could talk about how (the vote) may have changed their experience.

To the journalist, the teachers and former students were expert sources able to postulate knowledge-based insight into something affecting the community. But other organizations only considered people directly responsible for the vote as expert sources.

Nonprofits also rely heavily on civic organizations for news and sourcing. While journalists of all kinds of trust this type of source,[8] once again nonprofits seem to have an expanded, more liberal definition of this type of organization. For nonprofit journalists, nationally known civic organizations are a good source for news, but they also consider "tiny" local groups as civic organizations. For example, one journalist identified a local mission as a "homeless activist group," and another said a women's group that met weekly to discuss the bible at a local Evangelical church was a "go-to place to find informed thought." These are types of organizations, said one editor, her old legacy employer would not embrace as expert sources or originators of story topics.

When these smaller organizations create press releases, these documents typically catalyze news coverage. One journalist, who said they did not pay close attention to this type of group at a previous place of employment, noted the benefits of encouraging them to produce press releases.

> An example would be the bicycle advocacy group we have in (this city). I would bet that for a long time it was a glorified club that rode together on some weekends. Someone who used to work here asked them once about measures the city could do to make riding safer. They apparently had all these wonderful ideas. This old reporter told them to put them in a press release, which they did. We wrote a story about it and it actually made people take note ... This kind of thing gives us a competitive advantage over other places because groups like them know we listen to their concerns and they'll come to us with ideas. But why wouldn't we? Who is going to know more about what bicyclists face than bicyclists?

While other nonprofit journalists did not convey such specific examples, they did note that smaller, more community-oriented organizations provide better sources and superior story ideas because "they're part of the fabric" of the community, "know the issues better" and "aren't polished like the well-paid" public information officers working for a larger organizations. Essentially, these journalists are broadening the scope of expert sources to include on-the-ground advocacy groups. More importantly, the data suggests nonprofit news organizations actually favor this type of organization for sourcing and idea creation.

The journalists also expressed a decidedly clear aversion to "non-spontaneous events" as sources for news.[9] More and more of journalism relies on pseudo-events for news content, but a significant amount of the journalists interviewed explicitly mentioned this type of news source as an impediment for good journalism. "It's all so staged," said one journalist, "that I don't think I can ever get one legitimate good idea or quote from them." Other interviewees called pseudo-events a "complete waste of time" that should be labeled as "public relations." A different participant took this idea a step further and said,

I understand that if I cover a press conference, I'm making some decisions about what I include and what I don't include. But, however, with
that said, we might as well just run a press release. There really isn't
any substantive difference, you know? Everything that comes out of
(a speaker's) mouth is calculated and they're only going to answer the
questions they want to. The controlled environment of it all takes
away all acts of journalism.

While some journalists did not go as far as calling covering pseudo-
events akin to publishing press releases, they did make it known that
their organizations avoid covering this type of event "unless absolutely
necessary, like we can't do our jobs without doing that," because, in their
minds, rarely does anything of importance include, for example, a press
conference.

It should be noted, though, that while nonprofit journalists expressed
decidedly negative opinions about most forms of pseudo-events, they did
not see the irony of covering very similar happenings put on by their own
organization. For example, one journalist spoke glowingly about an event
his organization holds annually that includes a "who's who of everyone
that matters" in their city. He said that event generates "so many good
story ideas" each year. This event, of course, would clearly fall under the
umbrella term pseudo-event and does not differ in any meaningful way
from the many examples journalists cited as negative.

Orientation to the audience

All journalists rely on the audience both for sourcing and story ideas, but
the extent and the type of engagement matters significantly in terms of the
audience's agency in newsgathering processes. Previously published
research calls the way nonprofit news organizations orient themselves to
the audience analogous to "public service journalism."[10] For nonprofit
journalists, the audience plays a major role in news production, so much
so that many interviewees boasted about their connection to the audience
or talked about, essentially, a reciprocal relationship. One journalist noted
their organization's audience orientation as such:

It is an exchange of information. Somebody at a conference last year
was talking about cross-cultural engagement, and she said it's not
enough to say "I invited you." Or "I invited you and you didn't come."
Or "I reached out, I invited you, I engaged you." You have to be able
to say, "I invited you, you said no. I asked you why you said no. And
then I changed my invitation and you came." And that's the idea of it

being an ongoing conversation that isn't even two ways, but sort of like a partnership toward a shared goal of understanding.[11]

To create this ongoing conversation or reciprocal relationship, journalists engage in many routines aimed solely at providing the audience with more agency and incorporating them more fully into newswork.

The first way that journalists incorporate audiences more fully and orient themselves more closely is through open news agenda meetings. The vast majority of the journalists interviewed described policies in their newsrooms that opened typically closed-off meetings to the public at least once a week and, more typically, more frequently. For some organizations, "one meeting a day is free for anyone to come and join." The idea is that if members of the public are always officially invited to these agenda meetings, they will speak up and help guide journalists in their work and provide valued feedback. One journalist explained,

> As you probably could guess, it's not like we get a bunch of randos at open meetings. We mostly see people who are really engaged and care about what's happening. That's helpful in a couple ways. If I'm veering off path, they push back on my ideas. This can be helpful for where the story is leading me, but it also usually hints at how the public might react to a story. I think that's pretty important insight.

Overall, journalists talked very positively about having "different voices" in the room and people "who aren't afraid" to challenge editors. Most of the journalists said these meetings remained open and their organization did not promote them more than with posters around town and notices on the website, but some interviewees specifically noted that their editors personally invite some members of the public who they might believe could add to a topic to be discussed.

A major way that nonprofit journalists stay in constant contact and conversation with their audience is through social media. These journalists do not simply count likes or shares or just post stories, but rather see these platforms as opportunities for collaboration or crowdsourcing.[12] One journalist interviewed discussed their process for generating conversation and newsmaking on Twitter. She said,

> I might post a little bit of information on Twitter, just a quote from me or from another source. I'm steering that story, in a way. And I'm waiting for others to jump in the conversation and, you know, add to it. They kind of become the journalist because I'm providing a seed of

> info or a story idea and then they run with it. It's no different from a
> source messaging me a topic or idea.[13]

In this case, the journalist is utilizing social media as an idea generator, a place where they can brainstorm in a less-intrusive manner. For example, in this case, the journalist is not calling sources and asking them what they think about a particular topic; instead, they are just posting some information and waiting for the public to come to them and assist with the story. Numerous interviewees spoke of very similar processes, ones where they utilize social media to spark a story, gauge a story's interest or find sources to add to a developing story.

The next way that nonprofit journalists incorporate audiences closely into news production comes from the holding of community forums. Unlike open news meetings, these forums take place, oftentimes, at prominent local venues. The news organizations will provide coffee, a free alcoholic beverage or sometimes a pastry depending on the venue. These forums will be heavily promoted around the community and on the news organizations' websites. Sometimes the forums will revolve around a particular subject or, in other instances, they are general events aimed at understanding what is on the community's mind at the moment. As one journalist noted, the idea is for the reporters and editors to act as flies on the wall:

> Usually (my editor) will be the emcee, if you will. He'll call on people ask follow-up questions to the group, but we're all trying to sit back and just listen. It can really help find your footing within a story or help you get a good idea for the next story. You just listen to what people say.

These forums can happen at local bars, coffeehouses churches or other appropriate community gathering spots. For example, when one organization wanted to produce a series of stories on health issues, specifically food deserts, the organization held a forum at a local food pantry. They promoted the event at the food pantry and ended up having more than 20 interested people participate in conversations surrounding issues related to the topic.

Live events should be considered differently from open news meetings or community forums, despite the fact that these are also organization-held events featuring members of the community.[14] The main difference with this type of event is that they are not open to the public. These events tend include a cost for tickets – one that assists in providing a revenue stream for nonprofits – and feature a carefully curated roster of speakers. While this may not, on the surface, seem like a way to engage the public and orient the audience closely, it does accomplish this task. Audiences at these events tend to be from the community and they engage with the speakers and journalists throughout. Some journalists mentioned setting up booths at these events, booths staffed by journalists completely dedicated to soliciting story ideas or interesting comments from attendees. At one large nonprofit, these events can be expensive, but a journalist noted that "wealthy people are part of the community" also, and that sometimes these live events allow for "conversations with people who usually won't return" calls or emails. Fundamentally, these live events do not attract the same demographics of people that attend community forums, but they still do allow for interactions between other members of the public or audience, members that typically may shy away from conversing with the journalists. These live events provide a different type of community forum, then.

Finally, the last manner in which nonprofit journalists allow the audience into news production processes come from the comments sections on the organization website. One journalist said,

> When I started here, somebody told me to always check comments under my story. In my head, I was like, "What the fuck?" When I interned, my boss said never read the comments. Most places comments are, like, the most horrible examples of humankind. Here that's not it. You can really get some clear, quality ideas and feedback from them. Our system automatically removes the really bad ones, so sometimes you might see one which sucks, but most are either neutral or tremendous.

Numerous participants echoed that sentiment. They said that the quality of comments generated on their news organization's site surprised them. Comment sections often provided respectable ideas for follow-up stories. A journalist explained this:

> Now I read the comments every day, the day after my piece goes live. I'll check them out because someone usually will write something, like a question about something in the piece. That question will stump me and I'll be like, "Gotta get on that." I will too. It doesn't always happen that way. A story can be it, you know? But sometimes I don't know everything or don't think of everything and comment can be a like lightbulb above my head.

These comment sections provide another place for audience feedback. An assumption can be made that audience members commenting on stories may not be entirely the same group attending forums or open meetings, so, therefore, the organization is engaging with, potentially, another segment of the audience.

Application of ethics

Journalism ethics are implicitly embedded in most routines consistent across the industry.[15] For journalists working at nonprofits, these ethics play a large role in the routines they enact on a daily basis. Some recent research suggests that the influx of new market models could be impacting ethics, making it more of an organizational force than an industry-wide one.[16] This may be the case across the industry, but the journalists interviewed for this book would argue that at nonprofits, the ethical framework followed comes from decades-old codes of conduct released by organizations such as the Society for Professional Journalists. In one case, a journalist said,

> I received a code of ethics on my second day, I think. It was the same code of ethics we saw in a journalism class I took in my junior year at Syracuse. The first part was the SPJ code, verbatim and credited. Then (my editors) added some extra, more specific rules, I guess, to the existing list.

With the industry potentially moving away from a clear standard or set of standards for ethical behavior, the journalists believe that is not the case at nonprofits due to leadership. Numerous participants said that their editors were either also the founders of the organization or, often, started at the organization with the founders. Those founders came from legacy organizations and brought with them older normative rules. Essentially, what the journalists interviewed said was that because of the experience of their founders, first-hand experience applying traditional journalism ethics over decades of professional experience, there was a never thought about any innovation concerning ethics. One journalist said,

> (My editor) is old school. Everything is by the book. My employee handbook included a code of ethics. We talk about ethics at meetings basically every other day or something. You'll hear side conversations about ethics in the newsroom. They are just something always front-of-mind here.

While no other interviewee mentioned a code of ethics incorporated into an employee handbook, numerous others spoke of a pervasive ethical environment, one that included open dialogue concerning what constituted ethical practices and what did not. These reporters obliquely admitted that their decision-making processes are impacted by what they believe to be ethical. "It is part of everything I do," said one journalist about ethics. The other way ethics become something central to a newsroom is through the way editors and veteran journalists present themselves and communicate about ethics. For example, one journalist said whenever her editor faces an overt ethical decision, about journalism or running the organization, he will debate the issue in front of other employees, an act that not only tells, but shows other journalists the importance of ethics and the process by which it is implemented. This allows journalists to learn the right way to do things.

The other main way that ethics becomes a main part of news-making routines is through ethics workshops or industry-wide conferences, something that nonprofit organizations seemingly hold or attend more than legacy media. One journalist explained that in four years at a newspaper, he never knew anyone who attended an SPJ or the Online News Association conference, but at the nonprofit that currently employs him, several coworkers attend these events on an annual basis. He went to one only a couple months before being interviewed:

> Honestly, I never knew (journalists) had these events where we could sit around and talk about journalism. I learned so much from hearing other people talk about their successes and more so their failures. When you see what can happen when you do something, you don't have to make that mistake. I learned from other people's mistakes.

Other interviewees also mentioned industry-wide conferences, which typically host professionalization seminars designed to improve how journalists perform their responsibilities. But beyond industry conferences, journalists at two different nonprofits said that their organizations have hosted what both called "ethics workshops." One described this workshop as:

> We blocked out half the day and someone from a foundation, I think, led a workshop in our conference room. The whole staff, minus two or three people who could not come, attended. The speaker walked us through several case studies and we talked through different decisions we could make and what happen to us, the subject of the story or (this organization) dependent on what we chose.

The editors who scheduled these ethics workshops believed their journalists could learn and improve ethical application by practicing how they could while performing traditional journalistic routines. In effect, because editors have so much control at nonprofits, normally, they are able to implement traditional codes of ethics and force ethics to become a pervasive influence throughout the newsroom. They accomplish this in numerous different ways.

Objectivity

One of the most consistent themes that came up in interviews concerned a reluctance to accept the concept of objectivity. In much previous research into objectivity, scholars have found that reporting routines with objectivity in mind significantly affects news production processes.[17] For example, if a reporter thinks about objectivity as telling both sides of a story, they will not end the reporting process until they've talked to sources from each of these presumed sides. Even though this could create a false balance for the audience, it is essential to objectivity to provide balance.[18] By adhering to this concept, journalistic routines would follow a rather predictable pattern. However, journalists at nonprofits reject the notion of objectivity outright. They do not believe it creates quality journalism. One said, "Objectivity is dead. Not everyone deserves their side, especially when they're lying. My gig is about providing the people's side and making powerful people respond to the people's side."[19] The first part of that quote implicitly comments on the idea of false balance. The journalist is arguing that if you include "both sides" of an argument because that is the nature of journalism, you are implying to the audience that both of these sides merit equal consideration when that might not be true and someone could be "lying." More than a handful of interviewees pointed toward climate change coverage as an example.

> Objectivity in action. I say that about climate change. For years, journalists wanted to make everyone happy by giving all sides or angles. Then with climate change, the scientists paid by Exxon to lie get to have quotes saying it's not real. Those quotes usually come right after ethical scientists discussing real research. If I'm reading that and don't know any better, I would think both sides make decent points. Journalists can't include that stuff for that reason. It's our job to tell the truth, not both sides.

The other way that journalists at nonprofits reject objectivity comes through their allegiance to the public. As mentioned in Chapter 2, these journalists strongly believe they produce work for the public. One journalist arguing for the power of journalism made it clear that he is not objective; he is taking the public's side:

We can make change. I know that people want to say journalism is dying or whatnot, but I think that's bullshit, and I've seen it at my website. We've published stories that have changed policy and made things better for people. I cover my beat by busting my ass out there trying to come up with the things that would make everyone in (my city) better off. If that means more fresh fruit available, that means I'm going to write about fresh fruit and why it's needed, and I'm not going to allow the powers that be to give trite bullshit-y answers that don't say anything. They will respond.[20]

A handful of journalists expressly discussed how they considered themselves as siding with the public and not powerful people. For example, a participant volunteered an anecdote about covering the recent tax law proposed by the Trump Administration. He said that members of his community hated the law because it "enriched the wealthy" while "hurting some of the middle class." However, a senator in his state voted for the bill. When interviewing the senator for reaction, the reporter said the politician attempted to persuade him to write about the "positive parts" of the act.

He told me (the bill) would help (me). When I said it wasn't going to help the people I cover, he shushed me and told me I was being too negative. He said journalists were too negative these days. He even said I should make sure I put the same amount of positives and negatives in all my stories and this one too. I laughed. This guy doesn't understand I don't work for him. That law hurts my community and I'm going to take their side, not some politician's, who knows his vote will cost him his job in a couple years.

Journalists expressed similar sentiments when discussing how they determine how to craft leads for a story. They said readers should always "first learn" how a story "affects us." The use of the word us clearly belies some principles of objectivity. The word "us" came up numerous times when journalists included themselves as members of the public and distinct from those they cover, those they consider in power.

News values

When practicing journalism, professionals often look to established news values as a way to determine what is newsworthy and what is not. These news values "provide yardsticks of newsworthiness and constitute an audience-oriented routine."[21] Through the internalization of these news values, journalists can better formulate routines and understand what to cover and what not to cover. At nonprofits, the journalists interviewed volunteered three traditional news values and one that is the opposite of a traditional news value.

Conflict. More than any other news value, journalists at nonprofits look for stories that involve conflict, especially conflict between people in power and the public. The journalists want to side with the public and want to expose the conflict and potentially calm it. One journalist explained the pull toward conflict in this way:

> If people are disagreeing, really disagreeing, then we have a story. They key, to me, is finding the underlying reason for the disagreement. In my experience, what people say is the reason usually is not. The key is that the disagreement means that something is at stake. If that's true, bear with me here, then no matter what, people will be affected. That thing at stake is huge and the reason that people are disagreeing is huger. That's a great story and we need to tell it.

Many journalists echoed this thought, explaining that when conflict exists, it means the public is potentially disagreeing with each other. "I don't think that's good," said an interviewee, explaining that his job is to unite the public.

Proximity. Nonprofit newsrooms across the United States, besides one national organization represented by two interviewees, are overtly and decidedly local journalism. Some participants explicitly labeled their workplaces as "hyperlocal," but that word typically envisions a more myopic focus than many of these organizations. In reality, the data illustrates that these organizations tend to focus on an entire city, region or, in some cases, a state. No more. They understand that trying to accomplish any more could result in negative consequences. "We don't have the bandwidth to have people covering more than (this city)," said one editor, adding,

> If we tried to branch out to, say, (a nearby suburb), we'd be doing a disservice to our audience. We would be bad at covering (the suburb) and our now, what I think is excellent (city) coverage, would suffer as a result.

The journalists interviewed postulated that one of the main imprudent decisions made by legacy newspapers in the wake of disruption and drastic cutbacks was to try and cover the same amount of beats, but with fewer journalists. "You can't do it as well," said a participant. She went to explain that, in her view, if legacy newspapers simply tightened their coverage around certain beats, they could have still done those well. By choosing to spread resources around, all coverage suffers and people notice this. "We do two things," an editor explained. "We do politics and culture. We do those very well, I think. We have the resources to do those two things. We can't do more than that." Another participant noted that their focus on proximity is not only due to resources, but also because audience data shows that the majority of the people consuming the organization's content come from a specific area. "If our readership starts coming from somewhere else, I think we would explore expanding our horizons, but until then, no," said a journalist.

Prominence. Since many of these nonprofit organizations cover politics extensively, it is not surprising that journalists identified prominence as an essential news value. They consider focusing on prominence an extension of the watchdog role conception. An editor at one of the larger digitally native news nonprofits in the country compared focusing coverage on prominence to the way the press currently covers the United States president, regardless of who is in office.

> Back when I started in this business, most major newspapers and television stations had reporters covering the White House. They would travel with the president and report on everything that mattered. The number of journalists at the White House now is dwindling. We rely on wire services so much. That means people aren't getting locally tinged reporting. The *New York Times* and others have written about this. But what's gone underreported is this happening in state houses and city halls across this country. That's why we founded (this place). We have multiple reporters at city hall. We want to make sure we cover politicians closely. People should know what's happening by their elected officials.

This news value extends beyond just politicians to include local business leaders, activists and other community leaders. The nonprofit journalists view prominent people as power people and because of their adherence to watchdog policies, it is very important to cover these people. One reporter said, "If we don't write about what leaders do, they can operate in the dark. That's not right." The journalist went on to explain that they consider covering prominent people as a way to shine a light on practices, votes and activities that should be public, but often are not.

Anti-timeliness. As the opening anecdote to this book illustrates, timeliness is not a news element held closely by nonprofit journalists. In that story, a reporter found breaking news, the type of story that would matter to people right away. But despite an urge to break the piece, the reporter and his editor, together, decided to hold on to the information for a variety of reasons. Other legacy media in the area did the opposite, breaking the news, sometimes with results that could have negatively affected credibility. While many legacy outlets still put a premium on breaking news and timely stories, nonprofit journalism outlets do not, and sometimes exhibit a disdain for the news value. For example, one journalist communicated a story about actually uncovering a piece of timely, breaking news and bringing it to her editor. She thought that the editor would tell her to get moving on verifying all the pieces. "He really told me to call one of his friends (at the local TV station) and give her the story." That anecdote implies not just a laissez-faire opinion about timeliness, but an active aversion to it. For these journalists, they see their mission as explaining the news to the public and not breaking it. Some participants did mention working on timely stories and trying to break news, but the vast majority argued that regular people break timely information on social media, or newspaper journalists have that "type of thing covered." These nonprofits focus more on why the timely story happened.

Fact-checking routines

While journalists have always considered verification a key element of their work,[22] the rise of explicitly fact-checking routines is a relatively new entrant into the journalism industry.[23] In a sense, prior to the last decade, fact checking occurred before stories reached the public; it was assumed that journalists checked facts before publishing them. However, now, a key part of journalistic output revolves around stories or published work that just fact-check what, for example, politicians say during public appearances.

Many of the journalists interviewed from nonprofits specifically mentioned the election of 2016 and President Donald Trump by name as a reason for the increase in fact-checking stories over the last two or three years. "Post-truth. That's why they say, right?" said a participant, adding,

> We live in that world. I'm still in real shock thinking about how many blatant lies are told on a daily basis by this administration. I don't know if people are dumb or they don't care, but, at first, I was like, "Whatever." Now it's f'n galling. Lie after lie in person and posted on Twitter when Trump is taking a shit. It's not just him though. It's everyone who works for him and it's beginning to be every single politician alive. If they ain't lying, they ain't trying, I guess.

The journalist continued to say it is because of this atmosphere, that journalists are now producing more content aimed squarely at fact-checking. "Politifact and Snopes have been around," said one interviewee, "but now there's too much, especially at a local level, to leave it to two organizations to correct all the untruths." The local angle came up repeatedly, with journalists blaming the compulsive lying of the president and his administration for creating a culture that normalizes politicians lying and thus that behavior becoming pervasive across the country. It is because of this pervasiveness, said one journalist, that fact-checking is becoming so popular across the country and, specifically, in nonprofit newsrooms. "He (lies) and now everyone does it," said the journalist. Therefore, the need to produce content fact-checking of politicians and leaders is vital to the public. "I think when we do this, it allows the people to trace back the information and see for themselves the truth," said a journalist. They followed that up by arguing as many others did: That if done right, fact-checking content will improve the credibility of journalism because it can provide links to evidence, which allows members of the public the ability to fact-check the journalists themselves.

Beyond lies from politicians and other leaders, the nonprofit journalists pointed to one more reason for the spread of fact-checking: The amount of disinformation spread through the Internet, specifically social media channels. This reason is decidedly different than politicians spreading disinformation because those tend to happen in public settings and receive significant amounts of attention from journalists and the public. But in a potentially more nefarious way, people and organizations intentionally spread misinformation, sometimes labeled fake news, but this also happens in a less intentional way.[24] One interviewee specifically noted that "fake news" receives a lot of attention at the expense of disinformation having a more negative effect.

> Everyone's talking about fake news. It's fake news this and fake news that. I'm still not sure what they even mean. But, look, Russian agents or Eastern European kids peddling ridiculous conspiracy theories are something we're ready for now, I think. But what about all of these pseudo-journalistic websites writing bad stories because they're not paying good journalists? Or places like *Breitbart*, publishing things almost true, but with a racist spin to them? I think we need to pay a lot more attention to that because people are believing that more than they are Pizzagate. If a person is going to believe Pizzagate, I don't know if there is anything we can do for them.

Participants expressed this sentiment over and over again. Their argument revolves around the notion that the Internet is filled with information, most of it not fact-checked, and the majority of people on the Internet are not media literate enough to understand what information comes from legitimate journalism verified by a professional and what is just unverified information that could be true, but might not be. The participants noted that too often, for example, journalism ignores conspiracy theories such as Pizzagate because they find the story too ridiculous and unbelievable. Yet, since information like that can now spread easily online, it is journalism's job to produce material that fact-checks the issue before it can spread without at least "some resistance from professionals," as one participant explained.

Iconoclasm. Much research into routine-level influence catalogs media groupthink as an influence on how journalists do their jobs. The concept of media groupthink can be described as "journalists rely heavily on each other for ideas, and this reliance constitutes an important organizational routine, because it provides a reference point with which reporters can compare their own ideas."[25] The presupposition at the heart of the idea that journalists rely heavily on groupthink is that journalism is a tight-knit industry, one that features a tight in-group all working with the same underlying assumptions.[26] But, as stated in the previous chapter, journalism's identity used to be a stable one, so the profession's in-group remained easy to identity, but that is not the case anymore.[27] Journalists at nonprofits seem to actively disassociate themselves from groupthink. They seem to revel in what could be called iconoclasm, or the action of vigorously rejecting old norms or traditional ways of thinking. In a sense, these journalists occasionally thought about, for example, what legacy media would do and then most likely rebelled against those normative behaviors.

The interviewed journalists often hyperbolically talked about how much disdain they have for "the way it's always been done," when, certainly, many of the routines practiced by these journalists fit securely within traditional boundaries of journalism. However, two specific ways that these journalists struggle to avoid groupthink and enact iconoclasm emanated repeatedly. First, the journalists spoke consistently about thinking of their competition in "old journalism" and wondering about sourcing. For example, as noted earlier in the chapter, nonprofit journalists oftentimes do not approach the concept of expert sources in the same way. Some explicitly said they look for out-of-the-ordinary sources. One explained,

> Sometimes I'll try to imagine what (the local newspaper) is doing with a story. What I try to do is give people something different. People are sick of what journalism's done forever. I think they want to experience storytelling differently. This doesn't always work, but I imagine what (the local newspaper) is doing and then try to do the opposite.

This starts with interviewing people who will give me a different voice and perspective and intellectual contribution than the people they'll use.

Many of the journalists did not use such explicit language to describe how they avoid groupthink with sources, but they pointed to examples of incorporating more diversity into stories or actively trying to engage a specific audience that is typically ignored by legacy media outlets. By actively thinking about sourcing in this way, the journalists are avoiding groupthink.

The same or a similar argument could be made for story topics. The journalists consistently spoke about trying to find story ideas that "nobody else would touch" or would be "out of the ordinary and different" or would "surprise people because it's unexpected." While the outlets most prominently cover politics and culture, two topics also covered by most every news outlet in the country, they believe they seek out topics often invisible to the audiences consuming legacy media. Sometimes, this is due to avoiding breaking news. "The way we tell stories," explained one journalist, "we don't use the inverted pyramid so inevitably our analysis is something you can't get anywhere else." They also believe legacy media covers subjects in a very narrow manner, one that impacts what types of stories those places publish. The journalists from nonprofits believe their coverage is broader, intentionally, and this opens up more possibilities for stories and allows for more robust and different coverage of a particular topic. For example, one journalist likened this to making stories more tangible:

> Let's take a new law for example. The media will tell people what the law is, how it passed and, sometimes, what it could mean to people. They usually don't connect it to people. We, and I myself personally, try to find the little tiny detail that connects with people. That little tiny detail is usually ignored because it is little and tiny. I find it and it gives me a different type of story than everyone else.

The routines emerging at digitally native news nonprofits represent both the traditional communication routines found in classic studies of media sociology, but also represent new developing and evolving ones not present at many legacy organizations. For example, the way nonprofit journalists orient themselves to the audience can be seen as a manifestation of what many scholars and professionals argued for more than three decades ago.[28] As noted in early work, these routines significantly shape how news is constructed and the literal and figurative ways nonprofits are structured impact these routines in ways both seen and unseen, ways that must be further studied for their influence.

Notes

1 See Shoemaker and Reese, *Mediating the message in the 21st century*, 164.
2 See Shoemaker and Reese, *Mediating the message in the 21st century*, 168.
3 See Tuchman, *Making news*.
4 See Shoemaker and Vos, *Gatekeeping theory*, 51.
5 See Konieczna, "Do old norms have a place in new media," for a case study of one nonprofit and its embrace of journalistic norms. Or, see Belair-Gagnon, Nelson and Lewis, "Audience engagement, reciprocity, and the pursuit of community connectedness" to understand how norms form in public media organizations.
6 See Shoemaker and Vos, *Gatekeeping theory*, 54.
7 This quote first appeared in Ferrucci, "Primary differences," 205.
8 See, for example, Fishman, *Manufacturing the news*.
9 For more on pseudo-events and journalism, see Boorstin, *The image*.
10 For these two studies, see Ferrucci, "Public journalism no more," and Ferrucci, "Exploring public service journalism."
11 This quote first appeared in Ferrucci, "Public journalism no more," 911.
12 For a more thorough description of how journalists use social media in newswork, see Tandoc, "Journalism is twerking," or Ferrucci, *It is in the numbers*.
13 This quote first appeared in, Ferrucci, "Networked," 13.
14 For a good primer on journalism and live events, see Larson, "Live publishing," or Batsell, *Engaged journalism*.
15 See Phillips, "Transparency and the new ethics of journalism."
16 See Ferrucci and Taylor, "Blurred boundaries."
17 See Schudson, *The objectivity norm in American journalism*.
18 See Kovach and Rosentiel, *The elements of journalism*.
19 This quote first appeared in Painter and Ferrucci, "Digital marketplace," 115.
20 This quote first appeared in Painter and Ferrucci, "Digital marketplace," 115.
21 See Shoemaker and Reese, *Mediating the message in the 21st century*, 170.
22 See Kovach and Rosentiel, *The elements of journalism*, or, for a more recent application, McDevitt and Ferrucci, "Populism, journalism and the limits of reflexivity."
23 For a thorough understanding of fact-checking and journalism, see Graves, *Deciding what's true*.
24 See Tandoc, Lim and Ling, "Defining 'fake news.' "
25 See Shoemaker and Reese, *Mediating the message in the 21st century*, 183.
26 See Janis, *Groupthink*.
27 See Ferrucci and Vos, "Who's in, who's out?," or Vos and Ferrucci, "Who am I?"
28 See Ferrucci, "Public journalism no more" for how this is happening now, or Rosen, *What are journalists for?* or *Getting the connections right* for a historical argument.

4 The nonprofit market model

For one reporter, a particular story in the summer of 2014 proved problematic, or at least difficult to finish. The reporter, a veteran of newsrooms for more than decades, starting looking into a proposed bill that would affect health-care coverage in his state. The more he researched and the more he reported, the more certain he became that this bill would hurt the public.

"I thought, I have to cover this like I would any other story," he explained, "but, for the first time in this job, it seemed more complicated." The journalist understood that one of the driving forces behind the bill was a major statewide organization. Not only was the organization in favor of it, but had spent some money on advertising in an attempt to galvanize support from the public. In a normal circumstance, the reporter might include the organization's viewpoint and argument in his story and provide the counterpoint, along with evidence that would illustrate to the reader why the counterpoint made the most sense for the state.

Yet, as mentioned, this was no ordinary story. "(The organization), I think, thought of this as a potentially trademark accomplishment," the reporter explained.

And that organization indirectly paid the reporter's salary.

Like many nonprofit newsrooms, the one this particular reporter worked at relied on a diversification of funding sources to fund operations. In this case, a grant from the organization paid for a full-time health reporter, one that now wanted to report on a particular subject in a way that would, at minimum, frustrate the funding organization. This grant funding did not go directly to the reporter: Instead, the organization gave the funds to the news outlet, which then used them to pay the reporter. This arrangement, of course, would violate many of the traditional norms of journalism, but now many organizations are relying on grants of this kind. For this particular newsroom, the editor initiated a policy that any grant-funded reporter would directly report to the editor and never come in contact with the grant funder. "My editor," the reporter explained, "enacted this whole process so that they couldn't influence what I did." But, now, the reporter found himself influenced even if no proof that the funders even cared what he did existed. The reporter explained,

> Here I am, thinking if I do my job, I'm not going to get fired tomorrow, but maybe (this funder) decides not to renew the contract. What then? I would bet I'm out of a job because the (newsroom's) budget is pretty tight. My position, I thought, only existed because of this money. I'm like, can I write this in another way that's truthful, but doesn't look too bad to (the funder)? I didn't think I could in good conscience. I scheduled a meeting to talk about it.

The journalist sat down with his editor to explain the situation. The editor told him to do the story the way he would do it if no grant funding existed. "He told me to do it the way I wanted and I wasn't going to lose my job for it." This editor took a leadership role and determined how to deal with this situation. He notified the funder in advance that the story would come, but did not offer to let them read it or have any influence. The funder told the editor, in fact, that would not want it any other way. However, the organization's decision to accept funding in this way impacted newswork, at least at first. It created a situation that even a veteran journalist did not face in the past. "It never happened before, and it hasn't happened since," the reporter said. But it did happen. And while a grant funding an entire position may be rare in nonprofit news, varied funding structures are not, and they clearly open up new and sometimes unexpected ways that news production processes can be influenced. "That never would have happened at (my old employer)," laughed the journalist.

In the case of that journalist, numerous organizational-level factors impacted reporting on the story. First, clearly, funding structure played a role. But, also, leadership of the newsroom made the story end up the way it did. One could also argue, in a more nuanced way, factors such as innovation, market orientation or socialization could have also impacted newswork in that particular situation. The organizational level of influence examines "factors on which communication organizations may vary."[1] Consideration of the organizational level of influence is particularly important in current research on news production due to technological disruptions, which have "changed the nature of media organizations, restructuring existing ones and making possible new configurations."[2]

While communication routines focus on normative behaviors that are consistent, or at least prevalent, across the journalism industry, the organizational level examines variables that are decided by each organization themselves. This does not mean, of course, that all journalism newsrooms are completely unique, but rather that these factors are not determined by an industry. They are determined by the organization itself. For the purposes of this book and, more specifically, chapter, an organization is considered a group of people working toward a common goal within a structure of similar rules decided by leadership.[3] The data collected for this book suggested that several organization-level factors influence newswork at nonprofits. These factors include the organization's market orientation, the organization's leadership, the number of employees or staff makeup at the organization, the funding structure of the organization, the way the organization adopts technology or pursues innovation, the way the organization chooses to advertise itself to the public and the manner in which socialization occurs at the organization. For each of these factors, several journalists interviewed, at least, could point to ways in which their daily work could be impacted. In a previous study, it was suggested that with disruption, comes newsroom change and that "the evolution of news organizations could create seismic shifts in other levels of influence, but the catalyst for these shifts will occur on the organizational level."[4]

Market orientation

The concept of market orientation in journalism describes how closely a news organization follows traditional market principles. The concept was described and defined as follows:

> The successful market-oriented firm identifies a potential market opportunity, selects a group of customers that it wants to serve and develops a strategy for efficiently meeting the wants and needs of those customers. The central business assumption is that long-run success depends on a strong, organization-wide focus on customer wants and needs.[5]

Therefore, the more a newsroom thinks of its content as a product consumed by people as opposed to as a service provided by journalists, the more that newsroom would be market oriented.

The first way that market orientation can impact a newsroom is through its effect on content. Multiple studies have shown that journalism with a stronger market orientation sometimes publishes more "soft news" or, even, the details and framing of a story can change depending on market orientation.[6] As mentioned in Chapter 1, nonprofit journalism organizations tend not to, for example, commit resources to uncovering breaking news. However, this could be because of market orientation. Studies have shown the audience wants breaking news and that it is good for a news organization's bottom line.[7] Representatives interviewed from all but one nonprofit described their organization using details that would clearly classify the organization as having a weak market orientation. This would mean that because they see journalism as a service and not a product, the organization would not focus on breaking news unless it is considered as essential information to the public. This appeared to be the case consistently. Also, the majority of these nonprofits only cover politics and culture and do not expend resources on subjects such as sports and entertainment, two soft news topics considered to help boost profits. By focusing primarily on politics, the nonprofits are selecting stories that might not generate the most economic gain, but do potentially prioritize the audience's needs instead of wants.

Due to the weak market orientation of most nonprofits, the generation of profit is not at the forefront of news decisions. Therefore, there are fewer monetary resources to spend in other areas, including technology. While some nonprofit reporters, especially younger ones, discussed using technology to tell stories, many others also believed that the weak market orientation of their organization led to less innovation. One journalist explained,

> We're always looked at as this beacon of innovation of sorts because we do journalism differently and it's on the web. The web has been around for a while and we do very little differently than I did when I worked at newspapers.[8]

Many others echoed this insight. A participant connected the lack of innovation directly to cost. They said, "(My organization thinks) it costs too much money to innovate. I had one boss literally tell me that we just wait to see what works," they said, adding, "She said, 'We'll adapt once someone else figures it out. We're not here to reinvent the wheel.'"[9] One could also argue that because of nonprofits' market orientation, even if they are making considerable profits, they would invest those in factors such as staff size rather than technology because their market orientation prioritizes telling the best stories and not new ways of telling stories.

Potentially because a weak market orientation allows journalists at nonprofits the ability to not prioritize breaking news, the journalists interviewed felt they had more time to work on stories than their counterparts at legacy media, which are, clearly, more strongly market driven in today's economic climate in journalism. One journalist explained the difference between working a strongly market-oriented news organization owned by a hedge fund, compared to where she works currently:

Back before I took this job, I had spent 11 years as a professional journalist. I always worked for normal places that, ultimately, wanted to make money or there would be layoffs. My goal was to always beat the competition and that meant writing incomplete stories. I would gather news and have a scoop, yes, but because we had to publish so quickly, the story really wouldn't have the context in it, the parts that readers needed for the story to make an actual difference. That's how I thought journalism was. Even in school, you hear a lot about scoops and being first. Here at (this job), I'm encouraged to take my time. We want to make readers think about the story and process what it means. We want to be first with stories, but we're not going to sacrifice getting the whole story.[10]

The prioritization of reporting on "completed" stories inherently contradicts the goal of breaking news, which typically results in more profits.

The final way market orientation impacts newswork at nonprofits comes through the perception of autonomy bestowed upon journalists. Echoing the statements made by numerous journalists interviewed, one veteran reporter mentioned at other organization he worked at, he felt micromanaged despite the fact that it would be commonly acknowledged he knew his beat better than anyone else. He found the situation completely different at his nonprofit:

Here, nobody tells me what to focus on or what to write about. This is within reason, of course. But I can go report a story and then publish it the way I see fit. I don't have people shifting it in a certain direction or telling me to cover something that, in the grand scheme of things, isn't important to news.[11]

Leadership

In any organization, leadership can have a large impact on how that organization operates in numerous different ways. In fact, some scholars of organizational culture argue that nothing shapes an organization more strongly than leadership, that leadership is the driver of culture and sets the tone for numerous decisions across the organization.[12] Leadership is a sometimes-complicated concept in journalism due to hierarchal structures pervasive in the industry and the manner in which organizations are owned.[13] For example, many journalists might see the editor-in-chief of the organization as the leader, but in most legacy media outlets, that editor reports to numerous other leaders within the corporate hierarchy. In nonprofits, though, many editors also founded or help found the organization and therefore have power that is rare for a journalist to hold within a journalism organization.[14] The majority of the journalists interviewed for this book explicitly discussed how their editors could make decisions that would probably have come from a corporate executive at a traditional news organization.

In most legacy newsrooms, an editor-in-chief might have complete control over decisions regarding news content, but decisions about any other facet of the organization would be made by others, depending on the decision. In most news nonprofits, the editor would make decisions on news coverage, but also ones concerning finances, advertising, other forms of funding, employment across departments and more. A journalist interviewed said one of the first things she noticed about her nonprofit concerned how involved the editor was in everything.

> I don't know he found the time. He interviewed everyone. He supervised the interns. He decided what technology to buy. He scheduled guest speakers for the newsroom. He didn't organize the community events we held, but he supervised them and decided when to have them and where. He controls so much. It's a nice feeling because I know if he says it, that's it and I'm not going to hear something else from someone else in the future.

The more control a leader has, the more they can shape the culture of the organization. This appears to happen at nonprofits. As the above quote implies, the reporter feels like when the leader says something, it is fact. This creates less ambiguity and allows for, potentially, a more cohesive newsroom. An interviewee said that in his newsroom, his editor's ability to make decisions surrounding funding is, in his opinion, the most important difference from legacy media. The reporter believed that in legacy media, anything that can produce more economic capital will be embraced, for the most part, regardless of whether journalists believe the idea is good for journalism. But at his nonprofit, because a journalist is making these decisions, the quality of the work and "what the decision will look like to the public" is always taken into consideration.

When discussing the value and impact of leadership, journalists also discussed how an organizational leader who also is a journalist allows for a more ethical newsroom. They believe that the temptation to enact negative ethical frameworks typically comes from business executives running a news organization. For example, when discussing the ethical conundrums experienced when deciding how to approach grant funding opportunities, like the one described in this chapter's opening anecdote, one interviewee said,

There's never really a bad monetary opportunity for grants or what-ever, I think. The editorial side might disagree. The bottom line is it comes down to (the editor). I mean, she has such a great background with journalistic ethics that, like, the line does end with her. So basi-cally we have to feel out what feels right and then think about it. In the end, we ask (the editor) because she'll have the right answer.[15]

In that case, the editor holds final say on every ethical decision made by a news organization. This structure featuring the editor as the leader of the entire organization and in control of ethical culture can lead to many prac-tices appearing different than they would at a legacy media outlet.[16] One particular interviewee mentioned that knowing the editor controlled all aspects of the newsroom made it easier for her to ask for ethical guidance:

I don't know it's that way, but it is. I honestly think I'm more com-fortable asking questions about difficult decisions because I know she can give me advice and nobody will contradict that advice. At other jobs, not journalism ones, I would hesitate to ask my boss for help because somebody else would butt in.

One of the reasons leaders at nonprofits can affect so much of the organiza-tion culture is because these organizations tend not to have an institutional-ized culture. In one study about a legacy newspaper, the corporation that owned a news organization hired a new editor for the expressed purpose of changing the organizational culture and enacting radical changes to news production processes. The new editor arrived and attempted to accomplish the goal, but the staff rebelled and eventually the editor left the organization. One of the reasons found for this rebellion consisted of a prevailing organ-izational culture that could survive attempted change.[17] Since editors tend to found nonprofit news organizations, they can begin shaping organizational culture before there is even an organization. This can happen through hiring staff, choosing an office and conjuring mission statements that unveil the organization's purpose.[18] One founder explained,

I started (this organization) with a vision. I wrote down everything I thought we did wrong at (the newspaper I previously worked at). Then I listed those things on one side of a piece of paper. On the other side, I wrote the things I thought we could do to fix them. That paper became a guide when we started.

That quote implicitly illustrates how even before the nonprofit started pub-lishing content, the editor could impact the culture. In a legacy newsroom, the organization culture could be 200 years old or more. Therefore, the culture normally would already be relatively stable and hard to penetrate. The institutional knowledge in places such as a 200-year-old newspaper would make it exceedingly difficult to enact change, but when someone starts a news nonprofit themselves, they can partly determine the culture before anyone else even works there.

Staff size and makeup

The size of a newsroom's staff and the people that populate it play an important role impacting news practices. Those decisions are made at the organizational level. The data for this book found three specific ways in which organizational decisions impact this category: The size of the staff, the gender of the staff and the race and ethnicity of the staff. Nonprofit newsrooms represented in the data implemented policies, both official and unofficial, to influence those factors.

The size of a nonprofit's staff depends on two primary factors: Funding and allocation. The more funding raised by the organization, the more staff it will hire. But more importantly, newsrooms can determine the journalistic staff size by deciding how many non-journalists to hire. For example, one journalist who started working at a nonprofit newsroom the day it opened more than a decade ago, said,

> We try to minimize administrative staff. It's our policy to spend as much money as humanly possible on the journalism. The amount of administrative bloat at most newspapers is silly. You know about that with universities. The more you spend on the people not contributing to the main efforts, the less quality you're producing.

Since nonprofits, by definition, worry less about making profits, they are able to use resources that could otherwise go to business people for journalism. Other participants also discussed having very few non-journalism staff. One specifically mentioned how surprised they were to find their organization did not employ a clerk. "The boss answers her own phones," the journalist said. "It's incredible. Everybody does the little things." This decision, again, allows for a higher percentage of resources to be spent on journalism. Also, by not prioritizing profits for shareholders, nonprofits can have larger staffs. "We have more people covering our beats" than the newspaper also operating in the area, said one journalist, adding that the newspaper is owned by "a billion dollar corporation." Decisions about how to use funding determine the staff size at a nonprofit, and most organizations represented attempt to have multiple people covering each beat, something rare in many of today's legacy newsrooms. This decision would not be supported by the business stuff at many legacy organizations, more than likely, but because the business staff is small or nonexistent and more than likely reports to a journalist at a nonprofit, the decision is supported.

In the past and potentially still today, the journalism industry was dominated by males.[19] This might be changing today in terms of on-the-ground reporters,[20] but the leaders of newsrooms still tend to skew toward the male. At nonprofits, though, many of the founding editors are women and most newsrooms have a majority-female staff. At one nonprofit newsroom, women held the position of founding editor and the two main managing editor spots. A female journalist working there said,

> Where else could I find three strong women role models like this? Everyone that leads here is a woman. It's refreshing. They led where they used to work also. I get the feeling that if I do my job well, I could do something like that someday. It's nice working for women.

By employing so many women in nonprofit newsrooms, the cultural differences attached to gender could impact individual-level influences. For example, a newsroom made up only of white men could all see news in a certain light, while these nonprofits striving for more gender balance allow for more diversity of thought. An editor of a larger nonprofit said he makes it a point to seek gender diversity in hires.

> I would say it's important but funny. You would know this better, but I think the majority of young journalists are women because we always find it rarer to see quality male applicants. I would say our applications for staff positions run 3 to 1 female. That's, as I was saying, important though. We want to make sure our staff reflects the public and the public runs about 50–50 in terms of men and women, right?

Many nonprofits also prioritize achieving racial and ethnic diversity. They see this as far more difficult to achieve than gender diversity (due to the overall demographics of the journalism industry), but also potentially more important. Most nonprofits operate in cities and embrace covering the inner city. Journalists and, especially, editors, believe that the staff of a newsroom should reflect the community it covers. One editor said,

> My staff is predominantly white. That isn't a secret. If (this organization) covered, I don't know, Wyoming, then maybe what we look like would look like the place we're covering. The thing is we cover

(a racially diverse city) and yet we don't look like that. It makes it hard to make inroads with the community. How are we supposed to perfectly understand the issues if we lack people dealing with those issues or at least intimately familiar with them?

Some of these nonprofits, explained interviewees, enact practices meant to recruit more diversity in the newsroom. One journalist said she attends a career day annually at a local, diverse community college with a journalism program. "We're trying to recruit new staff or even interns." Another mentioned trying to solve this problem by publishing a section featuring "community voices," a section that sounds very similar to an op-ed page. The organization recruits "voices" from all parts of the community and asks them to write columns that could detail issues, wants, needs or more innocuous topics. The point is to diversify who is published on the website. Another editor whose organization operates in a less diverse area says his nonprofit makes a point of advertising for all positions nationwide. "It costs more, that's for sure," he said, "but if we just put an ad up on our site and posted around here, we're not going receive applications from all types of people. But if any aspiring or working journalist across the country can see that we need someone, we might."

Funding streams

In the past, journalism was often called a "dual-product model" by scholars because organizations needed to produce content that would entice consumers, and then organizations would sell the attention of those consumers to advertisers.[21] This concept made logical sense since the vast, vast majority of newsroom funding came from advertisers. For nonprofits, though, that is not the case. These newsrooms rely on a diverse stream of funders that ranges from $1 million grants from foundations to $5 donations from community members, to advertising, to larger donations from wealthy community members. Each of these revenue streams impacts news practice in some way.

While some journalism nonprofits in the United States eschew advertising entirely, some do raise a small percentage of their revenue through selling advertisements on the website. Three separate journalists from three distinct organizations mentioned that this sometimes becomes a conflict of interest at their nonprofits. For example, one participant noted that she believes her organization is hesitant to publish negative stories about advertisers. Similar comments were mentioned by the other two journalists. More regularly, though, interviewees explained that they are encouraged by leadership to use advertisers as sources "when appropriate."

"I don't call up advertisers and ask them for help on a story," said one, "but if I need a quote about something that fits the advertiser, for example, I go to them."[22] Another participant said they believe advertisers have taken note of the "extra publicity" they receive when working with his newsroom. "I have to admit," he said, "it makes me a little queasy that we use advertising clients as sources so often. We always mention they're sources; transparency is there. But that mention includes their business."

Nonprofits also rely heavily on smaller donations from readers. These typically come in the form of $5–$100 annual contributions from dedicated consumers of the website. Normally, these donors will receive a small token of thanks such as a coffee mug or a T-shirt. Many of the nonprofits researched consider this funding stream the most important. Donor names typically appear on the website somewhere. Many organizations, if covering a donor, will mention this relationship in the story. But some journalists interviewed said these donors can have more impact on news production than the ordinary reader. "When we know they donate," said a participant, "we tell them to call us whenever with story pitches or ideas. I think we're more likely to follow up on these if we know it comes from someone donating money." These donors to some nonprofits are also given special privileges such as private chats with reporters – typically through social media – or more invitations to the newsroom. "If they're on the high end of the donation spectrum," said a journalist, "the perks they get definitely amount to some impactful opinions. I mean, they can tell us what to do sometimes."

While small donations can be described as "the lifeblood" of digitally native news nonprofits, large local donations usually make up a higher percentage of overall funding for nonprofits. These typically come from prominent local businesses and families. While small donations can sometimes lead to access, nonprofit journalists argue that large donations definitely lead to access.[23] "We have people donate large sums of money and then end up on our board of directors," said one journalist. "The board makes a lot of important decisions about us." In a similar vein, a participant said,

> A large nearby university donates a big amount every year and we give many of their students internships. (This prominent family) writes a check and we really don't cover them even if we probably should. My point is this stuff happens. Maybe it's worse other places, but it definitely happens.

The most adverse effect this potential conflict of interest can have is that the large donations typically come from people or organizations that nonprofit newsrooms should be covering closely as watchdogs. When the newsroom could fear retribution for publishing something negative, it might resist the urge to publish the negative news. Some journalists remain convinced this happens occasionally.

They are similar, but grants from foundations are slightly different than large donations because while donations might come with hushed, off-the-record conditions, foundation grants almost universally require newsrooms to act in a certain manner. These attached strings typically affect practice.[24] The anecdote that opens this chapter, as an example, concerns a foundation grant mandating coverage of a certain topic. This is relatively common for nonprofit journalists. More common, though, are grants of journalism-focused foundations that concern some new "trendy" technology. A journalist said,

> The new rage is engagement, something that, if you ask me, journalism has always done. But we've been given a grant to experiment with two different platforms that I heard someone say "energizes engagement." I think, though, they really just eat up my time quite a bit and leave me with less time to do good reporting. But we're kind of forced to use these platforms at least a couple times a week because that's the grant, you know?

This remark approximates a common sentiment from nonprofit journalists: They are often forced to utilize technology that would otherwise be ignored or not in the newsroom because some funding agency would provide grants to newsrooms. The nonprofits need the grants, so they use the technology or alter journalistic practice.

The last form of funding comes from live events, something becoming more widespread in nonprofit journalism, but, at the moment, usually only utilized by larger organizations. As previously explained, live events are speaker series or concerts or something similar curated by the newsroom. Tickets for these events normally cost more than the average concert and can go as high as in excess of $1,000. These events affect practice because journalists cover them. One journalist said,

> Oh, man, (live events). We don't just cover them. I told a friend that we cover the fuck out of them. One last year, editors decided five of us should cover it. All five of us wrote stories about this event that probably would have been ignored if it happened at (a local university). For all I know the same event probably happened on (the local university) campus in the last year or so. We cover these things like they're huge, probably so more people buy tickets to the next one. It's kind of annoying.

Therefore, these events, unlike other funding streams, do not lead to more access for some groups, but do force newsrooms to almost become public relations executives for themselves.

Technology

What technology gets implemented in a newsroom is typically an organizational decision. The types of technology nonprofits utilize in journalism newswork can have significant effects on content. While nonprofits often receive the labels of "multimedia journalism" or "digital journalism," they tend to actually incorporate traditional elements of digital journalism such as video less often than legacy media. There are, however, three main technology types seemingly ubiquitous in nonprofit newsrooms: Source databases, social media and comment technology.

Journalism nonprofits do not all use the same source database technology, but seemingly every newsroom utilizes some propriety software that allows journalists the ability to search for sources and, in turn, allows the public to provide information to the journalists. Describing one such database, a journalist said,

> I call it a new electronic Rolodex. It's a place that I can go to and find people, but the joy of it is that it's not the same old people. It's new voices coming in every day, and because of technology, we can search by keywords and, boom, I have 100 names that pop out. I still have to comb through, but it makes it easier for us to find the sources. It's much better than man on the street ... This way, it targets people in your area who say they are interested in specific subjects.[25]

Numerous interviewees expressly admitted these databases make their jobs easier because they assist the journalist in finding appropriate sources who, theoretically, can add significant knowledge to a story.

The intersection of digital journalism and social media is fertile ground for journalism studies scholars over the last decade and a half. No fewer than 1,000 peer-reviewed studies on the subject can be found in journals around the world. These studies illustrate how organizations can make decisions concerning social media that have significant impacts on news production.[26] Journalists at nonprofits tend to all use three social media platforms: Facebook, Twitter and Instagram. Less than a majority also use Snapchat. All of these platforms are used in different ways. For example, Facebook is often thought of as a "conversation starter" or a place where journalists can engage with the audience. Twitter is more for promoting recently published content or upcoming events; it is not considered a conversation tool. Instagram and Snapchat feature different types of content, but newsrooms think of these as tools for reaching out to younger audiences. For example, one editor said Instagram, because of the people on the platform, can be interactive. "It seems to be a really good way to personalize our interactions with community. People will pitch stories there. And then people will tag us through these photos from other places in the community and that gets us investigating." The social media platforms organizations choose to implement and make a regular part of journalistic routines impact the audience a site reaches, the type of interaction with the audience, the kind of media captured by reporters and a whole host of other less visible decisions. For example, if an organization makes a commitment to Instagram, it often features a visual journalist all the payroll because professional-seeming media is "expected" on the site, said one journalist.

Few nonprofits do not allow comments on stories. Because most of these organizations believe engagement is an essential component of the mission, comments play a large role in how the journalists communicate with the public. However, these nonprofits each enable comments slightly differently, which then makes for a different user experience and ostensibly affects content and practice. The bulk of the nonprofits researched here have their comment sections powered by Facebook. This means that anyone with a Facebook account can comment on stories. "It's better than nothing," said one editor, "because it means we don't have anonymous commenters and those are never good." The two journalists who said their organizations allowed anonymous, un-monitored comments both vigorously complained about the situation; they argued that people could not consume the comment sections due to an "absurd amount" of hate speech. A handful of other organizations implemented more complex comment platforms that do not allow anonymous posting, but also need moderation. Essentially, at different times of the day, reporters or editors would moderate comments by not allowing ones featuring, for example, hate speech on the page. This process contained three stages: Users sign up for an account, user post and the system would automatically not allow certain programmed language, and a journalist would moderate the remaining comments.

Advertising of the product

The majority of the nonprofits represented in this study spend very little revenue on advertising campaigns. This is not a surprise in the journalism business since most news organizations operate due to a combination of people paying for the product or viewing it and the advertising revenue paid to them. In a sense, it would seem counterintuitive for a news organization to spend money on promotion since most aim for advertisers to give the news organization money for promotion. However, legacy outlets such as newspapers and television stations have clear visible distribution and also a long history, which means community members, on the whole, know them. Most nonprofits are less than two years old, and they exist only on the Internet; if audience members do not randomly come upon them or search for them, they are not known. Therefore, the organization's decision not to do much, if any, promotion can have significant effects on newswork.

Journalists at most nonprofits believe that the general public is, as a whole, relatively unaware of their organization's existence. The participants talked about telling people where they work and receiving blank stares or questions. They believe it is exceedingly difficult to amass a larger audience without better advertising from the nonprofit. A participant expressed this by weighing the pros and cons of such an approach:

> It's tough for me to think about. I love that (this organization) spends all it can on actual journalism. We have public events that get our name out in a minor fashion. I don't believe that works beyond a small, dedicated contingent of already active people in terms of media consumers. I told my editor once we needed to throw a large downtown concert with one national act and a bunch of local bands. It wouldn't cost too much. It would get the word though to people beyond the norm. I guess my point is that any marketing we do is always to the same people who are already likely to care.

That journalist's main point implicitly shows that public events concerning a specific topic do promote engagement and potentially catalyze audience participation, but overall a very specific demographic comes to those types of events: People already actively reading news and caring about community issues. Spending resources on events that do not even tangentially approach journalism could motivate another audience to visit a site or engage with the news.

The other opportunity cost of not promoting a relatively new news nonprofit comes in the form of sources. Many of the journalists interviewed expressed their desire to utilize unconventional sources or to avoid experts as much as possible in their journalism. While their reasoning for this decision is sound and congruent with the essence of normative journalism, it could also involve some necessity. Numerous interviewees, when not directly discussing sourcing, lamented how their organization's lack of profile sometimes made it difficult to attain interviews with prominent figures. A journalist said,

I can talk to the mayor most of the time. But sometimes he'll only have time for a couple (of) reporters and inevitably that will not include me because we're not seen as the authority in the city. The mayor even told me once that we do the best job of covering the city in a fair and representative way. That's exactly what he said. But, he also said, if he only has a little time, he needs to talk to the people with the most reach. And credibility comes from reach. We need more of it to really make inroads to the people we try to, I guess, watchdog of sorts.[27]

The above journalist worked previously for a legacy news operation in his city and therefore that experience may have made it easier for him to book interviews with sources. However, this could not be the case for the many younger journalists working at news nonprofits, journalists who said that finding a prominent politician who would take time for an interview was difficult. "A state senator I can corral," said one journalist, adding, "but if I want to talk to a senator in DC or a congressman representing (the state) in Washington, it's hard. A lot of the time I make do without."

Since many smaller nonprofits have low profiles not only nationally, but also within their own states or cities, journalists said it became harder to make an impact with their content. One founding journalist explained,

The hardest thing about starting (this place)? The hardest thing is realizing limitations. We've published some pieces that I think rock. They really do. If they had run in (the city newspaper), people would talk about them. TV news would cover it. Because of who we are, though, sometimes they're ignored.

The lack of impact some important stories have on the community came up often in the data. One could believe this phenomenon is simply a journalism industry issue at present, that journalism's reach is decreasing due to media fragmentation and numerous other influences. However, the journalists interviewed consistently compared the impact of nonprofit stories to those from legacy news outlets. As is the case in the prior quote, the journalists all believe their stories receive less traction primarily because fewer people know of the existence of the nonprofit. "I think," explained one journalist, "people might see a headline on their feeds and wonder, 'What is (this organization)?' If they don't know, they're either not going to click and read or they will, but won't trust it." Another interviewee echoed this statement more bluntly, exclaiming, "Who's going to act on our stuff when we haven't earned credibility, outside of a few circles, yet? You know? Why would anyone do that? They could end up looking foolish." In general, with a shorter past and less historical impact, these nonprofit news organizations exist in a slight cyclical environment where their lack of history makes it difficult to gain the public's attention, which limits their reach and ability to attain expert sources, and that, then, makes it more difficult to make an impact with journalism. Some of this, potentially, could be solved with an organizational decision to spend more on marketing, but that could also result in unconstructive consequences on the journalism itself.

Socialization

In his famous study of socialization in the newsroom, Warren Breed found that when new employees enter a newsroom, they tend to become socialized to the organization's policies, routines and, more esoterically, cadences.[28] These new employees observe how veteran journalists perform their roles, pay close attention to the behaviors rewarded by management and then model their behavior with this observance in mind. Through this process, an organization's rules, both official and unofficial, and culture are legitimized. Essentially, an employee will not become a veteran unless they perform in a desired manner, and when new journalists join the organization, they observe veterans who only became experienced because they did what was asked. Thus, a cycle continues. Therefore, the organization's policies "when established in a given subject area, is usually followed, and that a description of the dynamic socio-cultural situation of the newsroom will suggest explanations for this conformity."[29] This socialization process is a key to the development of the desired culture within a newsroom. It is also an essential learning tool for new journalists.[30] The majority of jobs do not feature overt training sessions where leaders instruct new employees on the intricacies of organization culture or the many established routines and normative behaviors desired. Instead, this information is communicated to new journalists by watching veterans in the newsroom.

The majority of the veterans at news nonprofits have long histories at legacy media organizations. Oftentimes, they bring with them, to the nonprofit, the culture they learned at their previous places of employment, which means, most of the time, new nonprofit journalists are socialized in older traditional norms.[31] This especially happened when longtime journalists began founding digitally native news nonprofits. A younger journalist explained the process:

> I started here four years ago. Back then, we had people who spent decades in journalism. I pestered them and stalked them to learn anything I could. You always hear journalism is a tough business and here

are these people who survived and thrived for so long. I'd be negligent not to eat as much information as I could.

The younger journalists interviewed conveyed similar feelings, but so did more veteran journalists, who often take pride in teaching normative behaviors to newcomers. Said one,

> I'm not going to be around here much longer. I tell everyone that. If we want (this organization) to stay (this organization), we need to establish some clear way for people like to me to pass down context. When I say that, I mean context about the history of this city because, without that, stories won't work. But I also mean context about working here and what I think that means.

Less-experienced journalists who started working at nonprofits more than approximately three years ago expressed how they learned from veteran employees. But some of the journalists who started their employment more recently, and some of the longtime veterans or founders of nonprofits, also occasionally lamented that these informal mentorship relationships do not exist anymore. One founder, who started the nonprofit around 15 years ago, said,

> One of the big changes around here is that many of the founding staff are retiring, so the place is becoming different. Some good, some not-so-good. I've decided to spend more of my time interacting with the new staff so they get direct feedback about what I want. The people that came here with me used to do that. If I leave, I'd stay on the board (of directors), but this could be a different place.

Some of the less-experienced journalists said similar things, noting the "lack of mentorship" and having to sometimes "learn about the job from someone who knows less" than they do.

For this socialization process to occur, though, there typically needs to be a setting for this communication. In the Breed research and other similarly focused works, the newsroom serves as a learning laboratory, a place where organization members can communicate both verbally and nonverbally about the norms and expectations of the organization. However, at many of today's recent nonprofits, the newsroom does not serve this purpose. Many of the journalists, the non-editors, primarily work remotely. Said one reporter,

> I would estimate that 66.666% percent of my working time, I'm at a coffee shop. I do my best work when I'm around people but not

talking to them. I can't work from home very well. Yeah, so I do a lot of writing and researching from Pete's down the street most of the time. My other time is either reporting from somewhere or in a meeting at the office.

According to most nonprofit journalists, newsrooms mostly serve as a hub for editors and a place to have regularly scheduled meetings. "I'm in the newsroom, usually, one day a week," explained a journalist, adding that they attend a weekly meeting for all employees and then occasionally visit the newsroom for a community or office event. A veteran journalist discussed how this took time to get used to:

> I don't know if you know, but I was a journalist for a little less than 10 years and then left to do something with a more regular schedule when my first baby was born. I missed the energy of the newsroom and so I went back. Since I came here, I barely go into the newsroom, if we call it a newsroom, and I have to admit, I miss the energy again.

Due to the shifting nature of who works at nonprofits, the advent of telecommuting and the desire to cut overhead costs, the process of socialization so vital in newsrooms of the past is changing, which is making it more difficult for organizational culture to diffuse.

In summation, the very manner in which nonprofits amass funding for their operations shapes news production in ways both small and large. For decades, journalism organizations differed very little in terms of funding model, and therefore looked and acted similarly in terms of news production. Nonprofit journalism is just one of many new market models emerging in this constantly evolving media ecosystem. All of these market models must be closely studied, which will result in scholars better understanding and isolating how specific organizational-level variables impact news production.

Notes

1 See Shoemaker and Vos, *Gatekeeping theory*, 62.
2 See Shoemaker and Reese, *Mediating the message in the 21st century*, 130.
3 See Schein, *Organizational culture and leadership*.
4 See Ferrucci and Tandoc, "Shift in influence," 116.
5 See Beam, "Content differences between newspapers."
6 See Beam, "Content differences between newspapers," or Ferrucci, "Murder incorporated," or Ferrucci, "Primary differences."
7 See Lewis and Cushion, "The thirst to be first."
8 This quote first appeared in Ferrucci, "Money matters," 432.
9 This quote first appeared in Ferrucci, "Money matters," 432.

10 This quote first appeared in Ferrucci, "Money matters," 430.

11 This quote first appeared in Ferrucci, "Money matters," 431.

12 See Schein, *Organizational culture and leadership.*

13 For a good example of leadership coming from multiple, sometimes competing avenues, see Ryfe, "Structure, agency and change in an American newsroom."

14 See Ferrucci, *Follow the leader.*

15 This quote first appeared in Ferrucci, "Follow the leader," 27.

16 See Carpenter, Boehmer and Fico, "The measurement of journalistic role enactments."

17 See Ryfe, "Structure, agency and change in an American newsroom."

18 See Carlson and Usher, "News startups as agents of innovation."

19 See Djerf-Pierre, "The gender of journalism."

20 See van Zoonen, "One of the girls?"

21 See Baker, *Advertising and a democratic press.*

22 This quote first appeared in Ferrucci and Alaimo, "Escaping the news desert."

23 See Powers and Yaros, "Supporting online nonprofit news organizations," and Powers and Yaros, "Cultivating support for nonprofit news organizations."

24 For a thorough discussion of foundations and journalism, see Benson, "Can foundations solve the journalism crisis?"

25 This quote first appeared in Ferrucci, "Technology allows audience role in news construction," 83.

26 See Belair-Gagnon, *Social media at BBC news,* or Konieczna and Powers, "What can nonprofit journalists actually do for democracy?"

27 This quote first appeared in Ferrucci, "Money matters," 434–435.

28 See Breed, "Social control in the newsroom."

29 See Breed, "Social control in the newsroom," 335.

30 See Schudson, *The sociology of news.*

31 See Konieczna, "Do old norms have a place in new media?"

5 The institutions affecting nonprofit journalism

A reporter believed she finished her story and submitted it, through a content management system, to her editors. After a nine-hour day, the time reached roughly 6:30 p.m. and the reporter headed home, believing she might receive a call with a question or two about the story.

"I remember this vividly because I only started two weeks before," she said. "I would venture to say this was probably my third story." The piece, a behind-the-scenes profile on a local activist theater group, proved enjoyable to report. "I had never even heard of something (like the group). They are part of street performers, part activists and most assuredly part crazy. That's for sure." While eating dinner in her apartment, the reporter received a phone call from an editor. "He told me the story wouldn't run the next morning and we'd talk about what needed to be done in the morning."

When she arrived at work the next day, she sat down with her editor, who was quickly joined by another editor. They liked the story and thought the reporter did a phenomenal job "capturing the spirit" of the group, recalled the journalist. "But they wanted me to add more what they called 'perspective' to the story." It turned out, before she started work on the story, an editor suggested – the reporter thought – that she could use a new newsroom technology to assist in reporting. The newsroom recently began experimenting with a technology platform made by a third-party organization, a platform designed to allow the audience more agency in story development throughout the entire news production process. The reporter's nonprofit newsroom received access to the platform through a grant from a different large journalism-specific foundation.

> I knew people in the newsroom were using (the platform). I got a little tutorial on it and really thought it was rad. Like, it could seriously make a difference with some work. ... But I reported this story the old-fashioned way. You know, you talk to the members (of the group),

some others who taken part in demonstrations and (a local politician the group influences). I even got some good video. I didn't think it needed much else.

But the editors thought differently. They told her they wanted some re-reporting and, potentially, some major changes if people on the platform suggested them. "I was told," the reporter remembered, "to listen to the community's voice." In the end, the story ran "pretty much" in the same form the reporter intended, but roughly five days later. The whole process, though, proved slightly frustrating. The reporter believed she delivered a quality story, but was forced to return to it only so editors could add a logo to the piece, a logo noting the reporter utilized the aforementioned platform during the reporting of the story:

> Let me say again, I believe in the mission or the reason behind (the platform). It's the right thing to do. In this case, to me, it was totally unnecessary though. I felt like (my editors) needed to justify having (the platform), which meant using it more than we needed to. When (one editor) suggested it before I started, I didn't realize I was being forced to use it, not asked. That kind of stuff happened often. I remember the whole thing so well because it opened my eyes, you know? I came to understand that if someone was paying us to do something, we did it no matter what. I've written some great stories that way since, though. We still have it, but I don't think it's a priority since the (funded period) stopped.

In the preceding anecdote, numerous entities from outside the organization influenced the reporter's work and, more generally, the news production process surrounding that story and the nonprofit organization itself. A new technology entered the newsroom and prompted a shift in how reporters and editors thought about storytelling. That technology originated from a third-party company. The newsroom adopted it through a grant from a well-known foundation. The platform allowed for a new level of input from the public. The platform changed how the organization thought about sourcing, believing the reporter's use of traditional sourcing to be inadequate. Finally, the organization would run stories that used the platform with a logo attached, a logo that ultimately served as public relations for the third-party company, a logo the reporter believed to be mandatory.

The social institution level of influence on news production includes the aforementioned influences as it describes social institutions outside of journalism organizations which affect news production.[1] Studying this level of influence can help researchers understand "the boundaries between journalism and other social institutions."[2] This is important because, often, when affecting journalistic processes, these outside institutions "enter into a collaborative symbiotic relationship" with journalism.[3] In this time of disruption, the entire journalism industry faces more influence from these outside organizations due to a renewed focus on audience participation through technology, a decreasing economic foundation that makes organizations seek out external funding more often and a host of other factors changing journalism as it's been operated traditionally.[4] Beyond these disruptions affecting the industry as a whole, nonprofit journalism, due to its distinct funding structures and reliance on many outside forces, is arguably even more affected by other social institutions. This chapter examines how nonprofit journalism organizations find themselves impacted by advertising, sources, the audience, the law and government, the education system in the United States, the market, technology, the public relations industry, interest groups, citizen content producers and, finally but potentially most importantly, foundations.

Advertising

In the past, journalism organizations primarily relied on advertising to fund almost the entire operation. For print journalism, subscriptions rates typically charged less than overall cost of the newspaper plus delivery; the organization valued the amount of unique subscribers, whose attention it could sell to advertisers.[5] But when circulation began to decrease and readership migrated away from print and to digital platforms, advertising revenue began to erode rapidly. Advertising agencies paid far less for digital spots than they did for ones in print. This led news organizations to begin experimenting with different revenue streams, but advertising still wields some influence over journalism.

Of the nonprofit organizations represented in this book, only about half utilize traditional digital advertising. Of the ones that do, though, some journalists noted that advertisers are treated differently than other businesses. Two journalists described discouragement at the prospect of producing a story that an advertiser could perceive negatively. "Nobody outright said don't do the story," said a journalist, "but I could tell that was the message they wanted me to get." More journalists noticed a different kind of special treatment. Numerous participants said their bosses encouraged reaching out to advertisers for sourcing. As noted in a prior chapter, these journalists explained that when an advertiser appeared as a source in a story, it was noted that they did advertise. Editors valued transparency in these situations. However, journalists interviewed noted that in the vast majority of these situations, the story could have featured a "better" source than the advertiser. This decision to feature advertising sources could have a positive impact, as one advertiser for a small, rural nonprofit said, the "reciprocal relationship definitely makes it easier to write a check for advertising to (the nonprofit) all the time."

Native advertising is the other type of advertising becoming more prevalent throughout the industry. This type of advertising, or sponsored content, presents numerous ethical issues and questions about boundaries between the editorial- and business-related needs of journalism organizations.[6] While the majority of nonprofits journalists interviewed said their organizations did not publish native advertisements, some did. Considering the content type's surge in popularity over the last handful of years, it would not be surprising for more nonprofits to begin publishing native advertisements. One journalist who does work at a nonprofit organization that publishes sponsored content said,

> The main problem with native advertising goes back to intentions. Advertising, it gets a bad rep, but in a way (advertising is) a good thing. It lets people know what they may want to buy. Without advertising, we'd all be using one product that's been monopolized or something. So advertising is a service. Native advertising though is intrinsically bad. Its whole goal is to fool people, otherwise it wouldn't attempt to look like regular copy. That's a bad thing. And we need to reign in such a bad thing. It should be illegal, frankly.[7]

Both of these types of advertising remain an influence over journalism content at nonprofits. This can happen through sources, topic avoidance or through content that resembles a traditional story to the audience, but actually should be classified as native advertising.

Sources

Media sociology scholars consider sources a routines-level influence due to journalism's reliance on interviewing people as part of news production processes.[8] However, when thought of as a whole, scholars consider sources as a body outside journalism which impacts work considerably. Sources have been defined as "the actors whom journalists observe, interview, including interviewees who appear on the air or who are quoted in … articles, and those who supply background information or story suggestions."[9]

At nonprofits, expert sources still provide a significant amount of influence on newswork. While nonprofit journalists believe that they avoid utilizing expert sources as much as possible, they do admit that many story ideas come from these experts. Therefore, while direct quotes from traditional expert sources are less customary in content from nonprofit journalism, these experts provide much impact through background information or story suggestions. Many journalists observed that many of their story ideas, for example, come from covering their beats, which frequently revolve around political institutions. This means that politicians speaking to an audience might say something that influences a journalist to produce a story. Or, as one journalist said, "The public should be in all our stories, but you still need opinions from the people making important decisions. That lets the public understand the reasoning through which important things happen." Even if an expert does not provide background information to a nonprofit reporter or directly provide them with a story idea, the actions of experts become the subject of a significant amount of stories pursued by nonprofit journalism, which shows that this type of source continues exerting outsized influence.

The other type of source that impacts nonprofit journalism potentially more than traditional journalism is the public. As noted in prior sections, nonprofit journalists believe it is part of their mission to incorporate "regular" person sources into their journalism. The journalists utilize technology and numerous other processes such as community forums to ensure that the public impacts news selection and the development of a media agenda. Several nonprofit organizations also employ mechanisms such as a dedicated telephone line and email addresses specifically intended for the public to use for story suggestions. Many organizations incorporate a link to these email addresses on the front page of their website. Journalists also promote these tools on social media. Finally, as mentioned in this chapter's opening anecdote, many nonprofit organizations retain digital platforms that allow audience members some influence throughout a story's creation. These platforms also typically allow journalists to search for regular person sources by topic. In general, throughout the journalism industry, the public is becoming far more powerful in terms of its impact on news. At nonprofits, the concept of engaged journalism, which explicitly allows the public a collaborative relationship with journalists is but one example illustrating this shift in power.[10]

The audience

Both categories of sources could be considered, in totality, the audience, but that minimizes the audience to only people who directly and individually impact news production. When exploring the audience as its own social institution that influences journalism, though, the conceptualization involves the entire body, whether they ever come in contact with journalists or not. At nonprofits, the audience as a whole most significantly impacts journalism practice through the organizational employment of web analytics and the practice of crowd sourcing.

Journalists at nonprofits incorporate information gleaned from web metrics in three main ways: Understanding frequency numbers to decide on story selection, quantifying engagement as a way to understand audience wants and using metrics to determine editing procedures.[11] While all three of these practices differ significantly between nonprofit journalism organizations and other types,[12] nonprofit organizations still utilize the information in specific ways. Most nonprofits do not subscribe to expensive web analytics programs such as Chartbeat and instead rely on inexpensive or free tools such as Google Analytics. However, even these inexpensive programs allow journalists at the nonprofits the ability, in real time, to observe what stories on the site are most popular by overall reader count or by amount of shares. This information is closely observed by editors and some reporters. Sporadically, then, these numbers will be acted upon and, for example, an editor will assign a follow-up story on a topic only because it generated significant traffic online. For example, one journalist said,

> Occasionally I've seen us do a story about something we did the day before or recently became popular. We've done that. But it happens rarely and I've also seen stories do well with the audience and then we don't touch the topic again because, frankly, there's nothing more to say.[13]

In a similar way, editors will move beyond just numbers of reads or social media shares and attempt to quantify "more central" levels of online engagement. For example, if members of the audience like a story on Facebook or Twitter or Instagram, a newsroom will classify this as a "low level of engagement." But, if members of the audience comment on the piece through social media or even the organization's own site, this is considered a high-level engagement act. Editors and journalists at nonprofits will observe this behavior and occasionally make news decisions based on it. Finally, these numbers can impact how editors specifically make decisions about the main website. If a story is not receiving the amount of traffic desired or, in the journalists' opinions, warranted, then an editor might tweet a link out to the audience or move the story's position on the organization website. Sometimes, an editor, if a story is gaining significant traffic or engagement, might decide to move it to a less-prominent spot on the website so a different story can receive more attention. While those are more macro editing decisions, audience feedback given through analytics can also result in more micro-level impact. For example, if a story is not receiving the expected amount of clicks, editors may change the headline to make it more provocative. One journalist said,

> I had a story that on the site with a headline used the word "sex." It wasn't getting too much traction apparently and another editor came almost running into the newsroom to tell the editor who wrote the headline how much she missed the mark. He told her to add "anal" to the headline. Apparently that worked because the story started trending hotter.[14]

Therefore, unlike sources who individually affect news production processes, the audience as a whole can do the same through numbers collected from analytics.

Journalists at nonprofits also rely on the audience as a whole through crowdsourcing endeavors. Reporters will typically "harness the power" of the audience, as one journalist described, by posting a question on Twitter or Facebook, a question meant to stimulate discussion amongst the audience. The reporter can then comb through the information shared by the audience and use it when writing the story. A journalist explained how that information can affect what he does:

> I can do so much with it. Typically, I'll post a broad theme. Then I can see what about that theme my crowd cares about. Boom. That's an angle. Typically, I find a bunch of angles that way. Then, I can even find sources because somebody in that crowd will make an interesting post or broach a topic or angle that I want to get into. I think this is an exciting way to do a story.

Crowdsourcing, like web analytics, gives the entire audience, beyond people directly speaking to a journalist, power over news production. Both of these are good examples of practices becoming more customary and impactful in the digital age.

Law and government

While the United States, compared to most of the world, owns an exemplary record of not interfering with a free press, "there is little doubt that governments of countries exert control over the media."[15] This control can come in the form of laws such as those pertaining to libel, or, potentially, cases concerning issues of prior restraint. In effect, the government and its laws can occasionally impact the ability of the press to cover some issues, especially those deemed related to national security.[16] In the rare instance of a news organization losing a libel case, the government can also enact penalties, specifically monetary penalties, which can cause considerably negative effects on staffing or even the ability of the organization to continue operating. These issues can affect all types of news organizations.

However, the government influences nonprofit news organizations in other ways. First, as nonprofits, these newsrooms avoid paying certain taxes. As one founder noted, "Without that benefit of not paying taxes, we would not exist. It would be impossible." Nonprofit status also means that these newsrooms cannot recruit private investors who could own a certain percentage of the operation.[17] But the most threatening way that the government influences nonprofit news organization revolves around the tax issue. In the past, the United States government, through Congress, openly questioned whether nonprofit news organizations deserved tax breaks, and the "uncertain tax statuses" of the news outlets also are threatening the viability of these organizations.[18] One founder mentioned this specifically:

> I don't believe that anyone will really try to take away our tax status. But when I'm planning for the future, this does matter. We've had grant people ask us if we could continue if our tax status changed. I think they would not give a grant to newsrooms where that would matter. It's scary. In the instance I'm speaking about, I honestly answered "yes," that we could survive. We won that grant. That was two and a half years ago. I don't know if I could honestly answer the same way today.

Other journalists interviewed very recently openly wondered whether journalism's perceived liberal biases could embolden conservative legislatures to change this status. "If they did," said one journalist, "I don't think anyone would shed a tear for journalism and they'd get away with it." This was a common thought amongst journalists at nonprofits, most of whom believe that their organization's funding model remained tenuous at best.

Education

The manner in which schools and departments of journalism educate future members of the industry can impact how journalism organizations operate. This can occur in the long run, with journalism programs focusing on a specific type of technology, but it can also impact short-term considerations, especially considering many nonprofits rely heavily on unpaid interns receiving college credit while producing content. For example, when assessing interns or the many younger journalists working alongside him at a nonprofit, one journalist lamented journalism programs' focus on technological training the expense of traditional journalism skills:

> I graduated college in 2005 and immediately went to work in journalism. I've been a quote unquote digital journalist for a little more than 10 years. When I was in J-school, we didn't even talk about multimedia. And I went to one of the best schools in the country. Seriously. We're talking about 2005. I'd been using the internet for like 10 years by then. But now we get these fresh-faced kids who know all about Pro-Tools and Storify or whatever's the flavor of the day, but can they interview someone? No. Do they understand the difference between journalism and P (expletive) R? No. But if I need them to cut a video, well, there they are. That's not journalism. That's an IT person.[19]

Many of the journalists at nonprofits with significant experience felt that the way journalistic education changes impact how they do their jobs. The journalists, like the one quoted above, believe that they can lean on younger journalists for help with technology, but also believe because of their organizations' reliance on younger entrants to the field, they need to spend more time training and mentoring co-workers who should, in the minds of the more experienced journalists, be able to do their job without much assistance. One reporter with significant experience directly connected this phenomenon to education:

> I've never seen a generation that needs more hand-holding. I truly believe this is the fault of universities. There are too many study sheets and extra credit things and too much coddling. Everybody deserves an A and, from my experience with my kids, teachers will do anything to make students happy. There so much less forcing students to think on their own feet and to figure stuff out for themselves. Now they get PowerPoints and lecture notes. They need to learn to adapt to a situation and figure something out. These kids in our newsroom, they just hover over people who have been around or their bosses just asking stupid questions.[20]

This issue could only intensify for nonprofit journalism. Similar to the industry itself, journalism education continues experiencing significant disruption. Anecdotal evidence suggests that due to external pressure, journalism programs will continue changing and, specifically, reprioritizing curricula design for undergraduates.[21] This, in, turn, will lead to younger journalists with differing skills sets and aptitudes becoming a large part of nonprofit journalism organizations' workforce.

Markets

When considering legacy media, the fluctuations associated with the market have considerable impacts. Businesses, which various types of journalistic organizations including nonprofits rely on for advertising, typically have fewer advertising dollars to spend when the market is down. The stock market kept going up in the 1980s and that led to corporations wanting to continue to drive stock prices up through media purchases. In effect, one could see the connection between a robust market in the 1980s and considerable media conglomeration efforts that followed.[22] That factor does not impact nonprofit journalism; however, advertising does to a lesser extent. But, more importantly, nonprofit organizations rely on donations from both individuals and large entities, donations that can evaporate in a down market.

Founders and editors at nonprofits often discussed 2008, the year the United States began experiencing the effects of the collapse of the housing market. This economic downturn and the ensuing effect on the stock market negatively affected nonprofits. "It was crushing," said one editor. "We went from feeling pretty comfortable to not knowing if we would stick around much longer." This depression particularly affected nonprofit newsrooms that relied more heavily on small donations from individual donors. One founder explained:

> We run the normal pledge drives, of course, and those can be a predictable source of a certain amount of donation. But we also rely on another predictable stream of month donations. If you don't count December and January, almost definitely because of the holidays, we also receive about the same amount in donations every month. When the market crashed, that changed quickly and for a long time. It was a struggle. We needed to recalibrate our entire business.

While grant-funding agencies and larger corporations with giving arms still existed and provided resources, nonprofit founders also said they believe the overall amounts given by these entities decrease in a down market. This can have significant effects on news-production processes because organizations may have to lay off an employee or, more likely, begin to allocate funds differently. "During that time," said one journalist, "a lot of the travel that I did for work became a no-no. We started prioritizing news in our backyard more than we had before." Other journalists said that around 2009 their newsrooms began caring less about utilizing new technologies in storytelling. But regardless of how many donations or grants a newsroom relies on, representatives said, an economic boom or bust can have lasting effects on the organization.

Furthermore, returning to the previous section's examination of taxes and nonprofit organizations, journalists at nonprofits said they fear more for a change in their tax status during periods of a down market. "When everything is good," said one editor, "they don't need the pathetic money we'd give them" through taxes, "but things get bad, they'll start looking" for money "and that probably starts with us."

Technology

Technology can impact news production at nonprofits in an almost endless number of ways. It is becoming a more and more essential part of journalistic routines. It's an also an organizational-level influence due to a newsroom's decisions on how to incorporate it. But technology is also a social institution itself, something that exists in society and can impact beyond any journalism organization's choosing. There exists a certain amount of influence from technology facing the news industry as a whole. For example, as society moved toward more of a reliance on mobile phones, it significantly affected how the public consumed news; this development forced news organizations to adapt to these consumption patterns or fear their reach dissolving. Technology innovations such as mobile devices impact society as a whole, but also specifically news organizations including nonprofits.

These news consumption patterns primarily involve a reliance on more digital storytelling. This forces nonprofit newsrooms to purchase more digital equipment and then pay for employee training. "You can't do journalism with video today," said one editor. "For a while, we let reporters use their phones, but after a certain point, that felt chintzy. We started buying some kits and software that let us use video better." Other editors specifically discussed the popularity of podcasts. The majority of nonprofits represented in this book produce content designed as podcasts. The preponderance of journalists interviewed said they either produced their own podcasts for their organization, or frequently contributed to more general organization podcasts. For many organizations, that meant a commitment to employing superior audio equipment. "I don't even know how many microphones we bought the last two or three years. They're expensive and break too much. So we keep buying them. You need them. Without a good microphone, we've learned, the sound is shit." Journalists consistently discussed the technology both their organization and they themselves needed for their work, equipment purchased by the organization at the expense of other types of resources.

Technology is not only used by journalists in their content production, specifically, though. Technological breakthroughs in society also impact the operating budgets for nonprofits. While many, as noted previously, rely on free or inexpensive web analytics offerings, even the inexpensive ones are becoming more expensive. Some of the larger nonprofits also employ very sophisticated analytics tools, ones that I've become accustomed to and need to update whenever the opportunity presents itself. One founder talked about the "great cost" incurred when the organization's website needed recoding due to changes in how Google search and Google News operated:

> All the old code became useless. It still worked, but we basically had a website that to the person at home on a laptop, it looked good and professional. To the guy on his phone, it didn't look as good, but still OK. But if a web developer looked at the backend, they would have said the website was from 2010. Actually, one of them did say that. That's why we hired somebody to change it. I'm no expert, but someone said that we missed out on maybe thousands of visitors a day because the coding was not current.

Public relations

For all models of journalism, public relations firms play a large role in terms of influence. These companies remain a driver for how journalists at for-profit and nonprofit organizations find sources and get story ideas. Regardless of the type of business or organization, they typically hire public relations firms

> to conduct public relations campaigns, targeting the mass media with news releases and media kits, setting up interviews or news conferences, organizing events, providing photos or video, maintaining online newsrooms and blogs, and generally doing what's necessary to generate publicity for an organization.[23]

While nonprofit journalists perceive that their organizations avoid covering the pseudo-events in the form of news conferences that public relations firms specialize in, they still rely on public relations missives for newswork.

Many journalists discussed how important email press releases were for story-selection purposes. "I can't be everywhere or know anything and everything," said one journalist. "At least press releases give me something to latch onto and explore." The journalists often mentioned signing up for as many mailing lists that originate in the community as possible. "I get too many emails that way," said one journalist, joking, "And after I cry about how overwhelmed the emails make me, I pretty much always realize how many good stories can come out of them." Nonprofit journalists carefully dissected how they use press releases, making it clear that they do not believe them to be wholly accurate or print any material from them. They stress that press releases provide ideas and not content. "That's big, the difference," explained one journalist. "It's not like we publish press releases on our site. But I'm agnostic about where good ideas come from. I don't care. If it's a press release, then fine."

Material emanating from public relations content also provide nonprofit journalists with some ideas for sourcing. The journalists offered that while many think of public relations as a tool funded by major corporations and aimed at promoting or managing the reputations of big businesses, all types of organizations use public relations to reach journalism. "Just yesterday I received a press release from a nonprofit whose sole motive is to protect voting rights. I didn't even know that (name of nonprofit) was even a thing." The implication of that statement is that the journalist used the press release to get a better understanding of the advocacy groups around her city and then expected to use the information for sourcing. "When I do a voting right story," she said, "I'll definitely contact (the nonprofit)." In that case, the press release made the journalist's job easier, allowing her to save time looking for sources when she begins work on an expected story. Other nonprofit journalists said they will contact known public relations firms for potential expert sources or for credentials to cover certain types of events. "PR gets as bad a (reputation) as (advertising)," said a journalist, "but that's not really fair because as long as you're careful, those people (in public relations) can really help."

Interest groups

Public relations firms and interest groups sometimes overlap, but these are two conceptually different entities and forces on news production. An interest group might sometimes employ a public relations firm to disseminate its message to the public and the media, but interest groups also interact with and influence the media directly. The groups are "involved in promoting their issue stance" and are "attempting to alter media content" or there are "those that do both."[24] These groups want to persuade the public and they often attempt to do this by utilizing the media. Many interest groups accomplish this without the aid of public relations campaigns.

The main manner in which interest groups attempt to influence nonprofit journalism comes through the use of social media as a tool to engage. Interest groups will frequently post on the social media pages of nonprofit news organizations, meant to stimulate public attention and force the news organization to react. One reporter explained how this can happen:

> What often happens is, and this is a fake example, the NRA will find all the big gun nuts on Facebook and then make a post about some issue to do with guns and tag everyone. This essentially gets the Facebook algorithm all aflutter. They'll also tag us in the post and then more and more people will comment. It forces us, in a way to write about the subject. Often we'll use those same sources if they're local.[25]

In that case, the interest group would be exerting pressure on the news organization. In other instances described by the journalists, interest groups will have dedicated people analyzing and paying close attention to organizations' social media pages. When the news organization posts something remotely aligned with the interest group's passions, they will comment with questions meant to let the audience know the group's beliefs or, to a lesser extent, stimulate follow-up stories.

The other way interest groups influence news content at nonprofits is through creating their own planned events that necessitate coverage. They will hold rallies or press conferences and inform the media in advance. "Many smaller people groups," explained one journalist, "will plan disturbances to city life. They know we'll cover things like that and have to talk to them." In those cases, the interest group will have created a pseudo-event, received coverage for it and more than likely also force journalists to include members as sources, which helps the group disseminate their stances. "They can get the word out themselves through some computer app," said one editor, "but if we cover them, they probably think it makes their ideas more legitimate or sincere and reasonable." Interest groups can make use of technology to affect nonprofit journalism, but are also, more than likely, sophisticated enough to understand how to increase their own coverage through actions taken offline.

Citizen content producers

Prior research illustrates how actors on the boundaries of journalism, actors such as bloggers who create content about news and media more generally, can impact news production.[26] Work from five years ago often labeled these actors bloggers or citizen journalists, but the ability to create content is becoming far easier and therefore more democratized, the more general label of citizen content producers is more germane. For example, in photojournalism, people who do not consider themselves to be related to journalism in any way can now commit acts of photojournalism that can impact how a news organization operates.[27]

Nonprofit news organizations place a premium on understanding the public's wants and needs. Therefore, journalists in these newsrooms pay more attention to the content produced by citizens on blogs or social media. This content typically impacts story selection. One journalist explained:

> I troll social media. Give me an hour on Facebook. Give me an hour on Twitter. Then let me have at Instagram for 45 minutes. I'm follow-ing people and groups from (the city) and trying to figure out what their posts mean. Once I do that, I'm off to write a story.

Another journalist, representing the thoughts of numerous others, specifi-cally talked about how blogs by community members provide a "huge help" when trying to gauge the interests of the public. He talked about blogs that just portend to a community member's private life will some-times provide a window into what events they might attend or their everyday worries are about. This type of content produced by regular people can catalyze story selection or even give journalists some ideas for source selection.

In journalism studies, the concept of metajournalism describes the different ways that content produced about journalism can impact the prac-tice itself.[28] Essentially the concept explains how journalistic trade maga-zines or articles written about journalism by journalists communicate to the public and the industry the normative beliefs about the profession, which then are discursively legitimized. One key area of metajournalism influencing nonprofit journalism organizations is media criticism penned by regular citizens. The interviewed journalists seemed very sensitive to criticisms coming from the audience, whether those criticisms appeared on social media or a blog. Potentially, due to most nonprofits' orientation to the audience and belief the organization must work in tandem with the public, these criticisms have more of an effect than those from other media or other social institutions. One journalist explained:

> If I've upset the public, I got to know. That means something is wrong. Don't get me wrong, I get you can't make everyone happy. But if there's a legit concern, a legit disparagement about something I did, I'm finding it and doing something about it. I think I speak (for the organization) in totality when I say that. We're going to try and make things right.

The implication of the quote is that media criticism created by the public will stimulate action on the part of the nonprofit newsroom.

Foundations

Perhaps no other social institution-level entity impacts nonprofit journalism as much as foundations. While foundation funding is becoming more omnipresent in journalism as a whole, nonprofit journalism organizations rely on this revenue source more than other types of organizations.[29] Foundations often provide journalism organizations with grants or operating budgets, but in return expect the organization to practice journalism in a certain way. Oftentimes, these foundations exert influence in the form of trendy journalism practices or particular forms of technology. As noted in the anecdote at the beginning of this chapter, some foundations will provide newsrooms with a specific technological platform and the newsroom will then drastically alter established practices so that it can incorporate the platform into news productions processes. Yet these foundations can also serve as a form of seed money, providing funds earmarked for new "innovative" market models such as a nonprofit, without the promise of future funding.[30]

Journalists, especially founding journalists, at nonprofits sometimes expressed regret for accepting foundation funds during their initial start-up. To the journalists, it presented false promises. One founder who understood that they themselves made a misstep recalled:

> We were given almost $2 million from (a prominent journalism foundation). They said we were innovative and we could be the future of journalism. I admit, they didn't promise us anything more in words or writing. We were only promised the initial gift. Every conversation I had with someone there, though, said they had our back. One person said, I'm paraphrasing, but that they were going to help us see it through. When the money ran out, no more came. I had to completely change how, well, everything.

Many nonprofit journalists echoed the frustration with the concept of innovation. They said that, initially, they had an innovative idea and received foundation funds to support the idea. The funds would deplete after a year or two, though, and when they approached the foundation for more funds, the foundation would decline and provide funds to new start-ups with new ideas. Said one journalist at an organization's founding:

> All (foundations) care about is how cool something sounds right then. Let's be honest, most of these (foundations) are run by journalists who

are (around my age of 60). They read a proposal with something cool sounding on it, and they're all over it. They spread their money around to anything they think is innovative. They're helping a lot of different startups, and that's a good thing, but a lot of that money goes to waste when these startups fail. Those funds could have gone to help support newsrooms they already funded. If I wanted to make sure I kept (foundation funding), I would have to reinvent this place every year or so.

This sentiment did not come only from journalists. Some foundation board members expressed something similar. They discussed how it occasionally feels like they abandon their own children when they fund an organization without continued gifts. "We birth these and then leave them to thrive or die. It can feel icky." Another reasoned that while funding recipients closing is unfortunate, the organizations do not understand the role of a foundation.

It sucks. I said it. It sucks when one of the newsrooms we've worked hard to support cannot make it. We provide this infrastructure and guidance, but sometimes it doesn't work and that makes you feel bad. There are people involved. The thing is, we're upfront with our newsrooms. We're not here to support you till the Earth ends. Our job is help find journalism's future. That means seeking out innovation, finding the model that will unlock journalism's potential to work with the public and, yes, finding the model that can become self-sustainable. You know, we may never find that. I don't believe it; I think we will. But our mission isn't to keep newsrooms alive. It's to look toward the future.

While foundations can impact the overall operations of a nonprofit considerably, funding from these entities does not only go toward start-up costs and operations. As noted in the chapter's opening anecdote, it can also support specific innovative practices. Recently, the bulk of these practices revolve around the concept of engagement and encouraging journalists to produce work in an audience-centric manner, in a way that makes the public a "partner" or "collaborator" in every aspect of journalism.[31] Journalists at nonprofits attempt to ensure they are closely oriented to the public, but still feel this "partnership" with the public negatively affects autonomy. One journalist observed,

The people are not as knowing about a story as I am. They haven't researched the topic. They haven't talked to a lot of people outside of social circles. I read legal briefs or other places' journalism. I don't think people do that. It can become infuriating when my bosses or *Columbia Journalism Review* or Jeff Jarvis tells me I'm missing an opportunity by not letting people tell me what to do. I get the idea, you know, but most people are ignorant or can't be expected to know as much as I do. It's not their job to look into something. They aren't journalists.

The idea that having a job as a professional journalist assumed some skills and ability beyond what a regular citizen owned became tantamount in numerous interviews. Journalists expressed disappointment over the way their "own profession" minimized their contributions. "If anybody in the community can do what I do," said one journalist, "why am I here? Why pay me."

Beyond the implicit criticisms, according to journalists, that accompany most of the engagement rhetoric communicated by foundations, the implementation of engagement platforms and practices also frustrated journalists, even the many who understood the overall point but disagreed with the application. One nonprofit journalist specifically mentioned a popular technology firm known for engagement, a firm that consulted with their nonprofit through some foundation funding.

Those people are zealots. When I closed my eyes, I thought I was at a fucking corporate retreat in Silicon Valley. All the corporate speak that came out of their mouths. It all meant shit. Seriously, it was like fucking gibberish. I want to say again, the idea behind (the firm) is admirable. I think all journalists aspire to much of the same ideas. But some of these people aren't journalists. They call themselves entrepreneurs and these (foundations) are giving them money that could go to journalism. These (firms) want to help, but they also want to make bank.

The journalists interviewed, almost every one, expressed skepticism about whether these engagement practices promoted by foundations had any positive effects. They believed that many of the practices already existed in traditional journalism norms. They also thought that some of the digital platforms supported by foundations absolutely made connecting with the public easier. But even after compliments, the journalists typically returned to the utopian discourse spread by foundations and the technology supported by them. "There is no evidence that this works," said one journalist. "They all say they have evidence, but when you ask them, they give tautological BS. It's like their existence is the evidence. I think their existence is evidence of good-intentioned swindling."

When considering the ecosystem of digitally native news nonprofits that began in earnest a little after the turn of the century, foundations have always influenced practice. At the beginning, according to journalists, this influence mostly came in the form of funds that allowed for organizational startup. That influence remains, but now, the journalists argue, foundations have extended their influence over practice, dangling much-needed operating funds at the expense of journalistic autonomy.

Foundations, as noted in this chapter, are just one of the many social institutions emerging as influences on journalism. As organizations, both nonprofit and for-profit, continue diversifying revenue streams, they open themselves up to more influence from other institutions, ones that may or may not have normative journalism as their main goal.

Notes

1 See Shoemaker and Vos, *Gatekeeping theory*, 76.
2 See Shoemaker and Reese, *Mediating the message in the 21st century*, 96.
3 See Shoemaker and Reese, *Mediating the message in the 21st century*, 95.
4 See Vos and Heinderyckx, *Gatekeeping in transition*.
5 See Baker, *Advertising and a democratic press*.
6 For more on this subject, see Carlson, "When news sites go native," or Schauster, Ferrucci and Neill, "Native advertising is the new journalism."
7 This quote first appeared in Schauster, Ferrucci and Neill, "Native advertising is the new journalism," 1414.
8 For an important primer on the power of sources, see Palmer, *Becoming the news*.
9 Quote is from Gans, *Deciding what's news*, as it appeared in Shoemaker and Reese, *Mediating the message in the 21st century*, 108.
10 See Batsell, *Engaged journalism*.
11 For a more robust understanding of journalism and web metrics, see Nelson, "And deliver us to segmentation" or Nelson, "The elusive audience engagement metric" or Nelson and Tandoc, "Doing 'well' or doing 'good.'" For more on this subject and nonprofits, see Ferrucci, *It is in the numbers*, or Ferrucci and Tandoc, "A tale of two newsrooms."
12 See Ferrucci, *It is in the numbers*.
13 See Ferrucci, *It is in the numbers*, 10.
14 See Ferrucci, *It is in the numbers*, 11.
15 See Shoemaker and Reese, *Mediating the message in the 21st century*, 121.
16 See Kovach and Rosenstiel, *The elements of journalism*.
17 See Nee, "Social responsibility theory and the digital nonprofits."
18 See Nee, "Social responsibility theory and the digital nonprofits," 339.
19 This quote originally appeared in Ferrucci, "We've lost the basics," 415.
20 This quote originally appeared in Ferrucci, "We've lost the basics," 416.
21 See McDevitt and Sindorf, "How to kill a journalism school."
22 See Barnouw, *Conglomerates and the media*.
23 See Shoemaker and Vos, *Gatekeeping theory*, 86.
24 See Shoemaker and Vos, *Gatekeeping theory*, 91.

25 This quote first appeared in Ferrucci, "Networked," 12.
26 See Vos, Craft and Ashley, "New media, old criticism."
27 See Ferrucci and Taylor, "Blurred boundaries."
28 See Carlson, "Metajournalistic discourse."
29 For more on foundations and journalism, see Benson, "Can foundations solve the journalism crisis?" Browne, "Foundation-funded journalism," Jian and Usher, "Crowd-funded journalism," and Lowrey, Sherrill and Broussard, Field and ecology approaches to journalism innovation."
30 See Lewis, "Journalism innovation and participation."
31 See Batsell, *Engaged journalism*, or Lewis, Holton and Coddington, "Reciprocal journalism."

6 Theorizing about disruption, innovation and future studies of nonprofit news

When digital news nonprofits first began littering the American media eco-system in the early-to-mid first decade of the twenty-first century, most industry insiders and journalism scholars foresaw initial disruptors such as *Voice of San Diego* as something to augment legacy media, not as the beginning of a potentially significant shift away from traditional America journalism.[1] Since the founding of *Voice*, though, the number of nonprofit news organizations operating in the United States rose from the single digits to the hundreds.[2] The democratization of technology bestows on news organizations – and specifically digital news organizations such as the nonprofits studied in this book – the ability to bypass prohibitively expensive barriers to entry such as television licenses, printing presses or distribution costs and simply expend resources, primarily, on reporting on the news.

Many founders of nonprofit news organizations in the United States started their newsrooms primarily as a reaction to changes in legacy media.[3] For example, one founder of a now-large Midwestern digital operation took a buyout from the newspaper where she worked for decades because she believed the newspaper abandoned its mission of serving the community; she felt like the paper's corporate ownership focused myopi-cally on profits and therefore spent too many resources covering soft news such as entertainment and sports to the detriment of the kind of public service news a community needs.[4] In a sense, the founders believed that their communities lacked a dedicated news source devoted to sustaining civic democracy and upholding democratic values. They started their organizations determined to provide the type of news that communities did not get from area legacy outlets. Said one founder,

> We need to fill the gaps. That, I feel, is the most obvious way to explain what we do (here). When you think about how (this city) has been served by journalism over the last decade or more, I would argue

it's been served badly. (The city's main newspaper) doesn't do explanatory or investigative journalism anymore. They don't really involve themselves with the community anymore. Well, yes, some reporters do, but some corporation located hundreds of miles away doesn't care about our community. (This nonprofit), we're all here. We've been here for a long time and we care. And our mission is to give back to the community and provide everyone with the essential news they need.

Studies of the content produced by digital nonprofits partially illustrate how these organizations accomplish the mission espoused in the above quote.[5] These studies not only focus on particular story topics but clearly demonstrate how nonprofits utilize different frames, different sources and provide more contextual information when covering the exact same topics as legacy media. Participants of this study agree: They perceive their organizations as purveyors of the type of journalism produced by legacy media during the industry's heyday of the 1970s and 1980s, but this time more informed and influenced by the actual people the news organizations serve.

Theorizing about individual-level influences

The findings of this book suggest that media sociologists and journalism studies scholars should consider approaching the investigation of nonprofit news differently than in the past. While prior work in this area tradition-ally argues for less of a focus on individual-level influences, research on nonprofits and journalism in general is beginning to illustrate why this is a shortsighted and incorrect decision considering recent changes in the industry. The findings here show that variables that previously had little effect on news production processes now do, at least incrementally, impact newswork. For example, for decades journalism embraced the concept of objectivity as a way to transcend individual journalist's biases such as political ideology; objectivity allowed journalists to implement a process that almost mimicked the scientific method and aimed for the elimination of bias.[6] This book's findings show, however, that at nonprofit news organ-izations, the political ideology of journalists is absolutely affecting news content. Very few organizations, according to the data, even attempt to pri-oritize intellectual diversity, amassing instead staffs almost entirely made up of avowed liberal journalists. These nonprofits tend to have flattened hierarchal structures, which means fewer total editors and less oversight on reporters. This means that reporters are able to wield far more agency over story choices, which can lead to the anecdote shared earlier in the book of the reporter seeking out stories concerning climate change due to a personal connection to the story and an individual belief in the topic's importance. In one of the earliest studies of gatekeeping, David Manning White researched "Mr. Gates," a wire editor at a Midwestern newspaper who, for example, did not like the Catholic Church and therefore chose not to publish positive stories about the religious organization.[7] White argued this illustrated how individuals controlled the gates of information, but subsequent scholars have criticized White's early work because of its lack of consideration of other influences on Mr. Gates.[8] While those criticisms remain absolutely appropriate, the power of individual journalists at smaller nonprofit newsrooms is growing and unmatched in the vast majority of legacy media outlets.

One way in which in individual journalists can impact news construction is through their professional identities. Early work found that journalistic identity remained rather stable over the years;[9] however, more recent scholarship has found that journalists at digital news outlets, which include the majority of nonprofits, discursively conceive their identities in ways functionally disparate to traditional journalists.[10] This morphing identity construction alludes to the potentially sizable impact of individual journalists on news production. For example, if nonprofit journalists see themselves as definitively different to traditional journalists, then they will act differently, which will undoubtedly affect news content. This could very well happen often at nonprofits since they are, as noted previously in this chapter, often founded in clear contradistinction to legacy media. Nonprofit founders start their organizations because they want to be different from legacy media and subsequently imbue that feeling into their employees, who then internalize the very mission of acting differently in their profession. Journalistic professional identity is often most inherent in role conception, or the way that journalists conceive their professional roles.[11] This book's best example of the difference between nonprofits and legacy media comes in the illumination of a new role conception: The community advocate. While previous literature introduced similar role conceptions such as the populist mobilizer, the community advocate role is distinct in its conception of the journalist as intrinsically part of the community. The populist mobilizer role, which scholars highlighted after movements such as public journalism, revolves around the idea of giving voice to ordinary citizens and providing entertainment as part of the job.[12] Implicit in that definition is journalists letting ordinary people into news production processes, but the community advocate role does not argue for letting ordinary people in because the reporter is already a member of the community. Due to norms such as objectivity, advocacy is often frowned upon in journalism, but this is becoming a less prevalent opinion throughout the industry,[13] and nonprofit news organizations almost entirely embrace the idea of advocacy journalism aimed at bettering the community.

While it might sound positive that nonprofit news organizations are, by and large, ignoring outdated and misinterpreted norms such as objectivity, if individual characteristics such as political ideology or other personal values are having more of an impact on news production, it could lead to journalists believing their opinions and values are what is good for the community, regardless of whether that is accurate or not. Therefore, while the idea of advocating for the community is, theoretically, a positive development that tangibly illustrates a loyalty to citizens above all else, how this role is enacted is key. If, for example, a nonprofit organization truly prioritizes understanding the community's needs, it can enact the role of community advocate in a way that can have significant positive effects.

Theorizing about routines-level influences

In the macro sense, the act of reporting – and the routines inherent in that act – remains relatively the same at journalistic nonprofits. However, when examining these routines on the micro level, this book's data begin to illustrate how small routine changes can have large effects. For example, most early work in this area found that journalists rely on groupthink, which is another way of arguing that journalists look to each other when determining what is news. In a sense, at legacy media, journalism influences other journalism. And while this partially still happens at digital nonprofits, a key contribution of this book is the idea of iconoclasm, or the act of enthusiastically rejecting the traditional norms of journalism. At nonprofits, according to the participants, many journalists intentionally attempt to distance themselves from legacy media by acting in ways they perceive as the antithesis to what happens at traditional news organizations. "The way I look at it," said one reporter at a nonprofit in a city with two legacy newspapers, "if (those newspapers) do it one way, I want to do it another. Why wouldn't I? They are failing to do what news should, so I'm not going to kowtow to that way of acting." By actively disassociating themselves from those normative ideals, journalists at nonprofits then begin to enact new communication routines that will inevitable impact news production processes.

These new communication routines primarily can be understood by thinking about how nonprofit journalists orient themselves to both sources and the audience. It is this way that they separate themselves from legacy media. While the industry as a whole now avows ideas such as engagement or what some scholars reciprocal journalism,[14] early research into the area shows that while journalists and leaders at legacy media may talk about these ideas, they typically do not actually pursue them or apply them.[15] However, at nonprofits, journalists orient themselves strongly to their audience.[16] As part of their routines, nonprofit journalists participate in numerous practices that create what some participants called an ongoing conversation between journalists and the audience. By, for example, having open news meetings that provide the audience with an opportunity to comment on or steer stories before publication, journalists at nonprofits are incorporating audience feedback in ways that most legacy outlets do not. These practices, potentially, create more engagement and allow nonprofits to practice a form of public service journalism that accomplishes many goals set by legacy media decades ago, but not accomplished for a variety of reasons.[17]

While nonprofit journalism's orientation to its audience is, arguably, considerably different from the legacy media orientation, as noted, the latter at least publicly avow similar thought. So, therefore, while nonprofits are enacting different practices, these are not revolutionary and some legacy outlets do the same in some manner. However, the way nonprofit organizations orient to sources should be considered significantly different. By defining the term "expert source" at least slightly differently, journalists at nonprofits consider a far more diverse range of sources when constructing news. Numerous journalists interviewed for this book explicitly discussed the need to avoid traditional expert sources such as politicians unless absolutely necessary. These journalists argue that these traditional expert sources are too trained to provide quality information and not enough a part of the actual community to accurately represent the community's needs. This does not, of course, mean that nonprofit organizations do not utilize politicians in stories, but rather the idea of who is an expert source is significantly broader at nonprofits. This altered definition manifests itself in nonprofit journalists performing communication routines aimed at incorporating different types of sources in stories. This can result in far more contextualized or citizen-centric stories about traditional topics such as a local murder.[18]

Finally, nonprofit organizations define news in slightly different ways to legacy outlets. Legacy media, in this age of fragmentation and more competition for eyeballs, is more and more prioritizing breaking news.[19] This priority aligns closely with the traditional news value of timeliness. However, this book illustrates how nonprofit organizations actually have an anti-timeliness news value. More than likely due, for many reasons, to an inability to effectively break news as successfully as legacy media, and a need to distinguish themselves from legacy media – another example of iconoclasm – nonprofit outlets prioritize contextualizing and analyzing stories, not breaking them. The opening anecdote to this book illustrated how a reporter at a nonprofit held a big story that, if broken, would have resulted in the kind of attention that legacy media crave. However, the reporter – and the organization – believed the most positive course of action was not to publish a short piece of breaking news, but rather a longer contextualized piece featuring more reporting, a piece that, according to the editor, "the community could truly use."

Theorizing about organizational-level influences

Similar to many non-legacy market models of journalism, nonprofits often lack what would be considered a traditional newsroom.[20] This can have an influence on news construction in a variety of ways. First, the special setup of a newsroom can impact on how journalists do their jobs and perceive their role.[21] More importantly, arguably, a centralized newsroom can assist in the process of socialization, something eminently important in terms of communicating journalistic norms.[22] Without a traditional newsroom, less socialization happens and, again, individual influences can have more of an effect. For example, if a journalist owns a specific bias that can manifest itself in the news, if they worked in a traditional newsroom, they might observe how veteran journalists avoid or resist that bias. They might also be explicitly told by veterans that the bias needs to eradicated from coverage. However, without a newsroom, some socialization cannot happen as it does in most legacy organizations.

Theories of organizational culture and communication strongly argue that no variable affects how an organization operates more than leadership.[23] At legacy media organizations, leadership can offer a distinctly stratified and oblique hierarchy. Most legacy outlets are owned by a public corporation, which gives shareholders – or the traditional desires of shareholders – a significant influence on the news organization. However, there are also corporate CEOs, presidents of news divisions and other leaders who often never step foot in the news organization. Then, at the actual news organization, there are numerous departments and titles that have some sway over an editor in chief, the person typically running the news operation. However, as previously noted, journalists founded most nonprofits and, because of the unique structure of nonprofit organizations, typically stay in charge. While there is a board of advisors at most nonprofit news organizations, the founding journalists typically hold the most power over how the newsroom and overall organization runs. This is a sharp difference from legacy media. And if, as noted, leadership plays an outsized role in developing organizational culture, mission and enacted processes, then news organizations such as nonprofits that are actually run by journalists will operate quite differently than ones overseen by a corporate CEO also managing numerous other companies. This structure is in place at the vast majority of digitally native news nonprofits in the United States and leads to a journalism-centric enterprise. For example, participants often noted how even the most controversial decisions would be made by their editors without needing to check with anyone outside of the newsroom. This means the values of news are prioritized over the values of, for example, business.

The majority of news nonprofits, most notably because of their non-profit status, operate with what scholars would call a weak market orientation.[24] The stronger a market orientation, the more that organizations prioritizes traditional market values such as profit. In journalism, a strong market orientation can lead to market-driven journalism, which prioritizes providing readers with what they want, not what they need.[25] Without focusing on profit and thinking of news as a product rather than a service, nonprofit organizations are free to emphasize the kind of journalism they think most assists with community building. This book's data and other studies show that market orientation can also have significant effects on journalistic routines; for example, organizations of differing market orientations incorporate web analytics into news routines differently.[26] However, while having a weak market orientation allows these digital nonprofits more agency in terms of coverage choices and the type of news published, a potential negative result could be happening. When considering the intersection of market orientation and nonprofits, conventional theorizing would argue that not having to prioritize the type of stories that typically garner eyeballs such as sports or entertainment would result in a more civic-focused news organization that truly treats news as a service and not a product. Yet, as previously noted, journalists at nonprofits are very closely oriented to the public or the audience. They engage the audience constantly and enact processes and routines expressly for the purpose of giving the audience far more agency in coverage choices. Unintentionally, then, nonprofit news organizations could be implicitly enacting market-driven journalism, a type of journalism wholly criticized by journalists. But if market-driven journalism focuses on giving audiences what they want, how does it differ from nonprofit journalism organizations fundamentally and constantly asking the audience what it wants in a variety of different manners?

Theorizing about social institution-level influences

While this book illustrated how various influences at different levels of analysis could be unique, or close to it, at nonprofit organizations, the findings suggest that social institution-level influences might be the most robust. In effect, digitally native news nonprofits allow various social institutions undue influence over news construction, institutions almost completely ignored by legacy media. Scholar Edwin Baker argued that journalism functioned as a dual-product model, one that needed to please audiences to gather attention, but also one that then needed to sell that attention to advertisers.[27] Essentially, unlike, say, a company that manufacturers stereos and only needs to interest consumers, journalism organizations need to interest consumers but then also advertisers. Baker's position was that, both implicitly and explicitly, advertising – a social institution – affects journalism in a very significant way. Because most journalism nonprofits eschew advertising or utilize very little of it, many studies implicitly argue that nonprofit journalism can get closer to the ideal form of normative journalism without having to worry about advertising or, more generally, a profit.[28] However, this argument ignores how nonprofits rely heavily on foundation funding, which acts in a similar manner to advertising. But, as noted in journalism scholarship,[29] journalism organizations have, over time, enacted the metaphorical but oftentimes literal idea of a wall between the news side of the organization and the business side of the organization. This illustrates how the journalism industry, historically, manifestly attempted to eliminate or, at least, minimize, any influence advertising had on journalistic processes. But nonprofits often rely on foundations for funding, foundations such as the Knight Foundation. These foundations oftentimes provide funding based on particular "innovative" ideas. Because nonprofits rely on this funding, they often, as noted in a prior chapter, propose to enact practices they believe will secure them funding. For example, one participant discussed how his organization put together a grant proposal that promised to prioritize virtual reality storytelling since that is what the funding foundation wanted. The news nonprofit did not have any experience in virtual reality, but would have gladly started utilizing the technology if the foundation chose them for a grant. Therefore, while news organizations have always tried to eliminate influence from advertising, they do the opposite with foundation funding, seeking it out with the expressed promise to let the foundation impact news.

Potentially more benignly, these foundations or grant-providers fund entire beats at some news nonprofits. These beats might not exist if not for the funding. Consequently, it can be convincingly argued that, again, nonprofits are seeking out grants that put coverage decisions in the hands of foundations or grant-giving organizations as opposed to the journalists. To juxtapose this with advertising, it is easy to argue that this is similar to, for example, Philip Morris International funding a health reporter or Toyota only advertising with a newspaper if all the reporters drove Toyota models.

In either of those cases, journalists and scholars would contend that this was not ethical or normative behavior, but foundation funding seems to have become an integral part of nonprofit journalism.

In a similar manner, technology companies have become influencers of journalism in a way that did not occur in the past. Yes, journalism always existed as a technology-focused industry, one where technological disruptions such as television impact the industry and its practices. However, those influences were indirect and more of a function of how society embraced various forms of technology. At nonprofits in the United States, technology companies such as Google or platforms such as Hearken now have direct influence on journalistic practice. These companies provide journalism organizations with products that oftentimes come with strings attached. For example, Hearken provides a platform that helps to facilitate engagement. Regardless of the accuracy of this claim, the company's service, numerous interviewed journalists said, impacts how they report on a story. There is a clear pattern that must be followed and the technology itself catalyzes particular practices. As one journalist noted, "Depending on what's engagement really, it might be good or it might not. I know, you know, that once we embraced Hearken, the way I do my thing changed. That's unambiguous." Therefore, it's clear that technology such as Hearken does not indirectly impact practice, such as the invention of television, but rather directly impacts it, with the full authorization of the news organization.

An argument for a new hierarchy

While the following theoretical argument should and will be augmented with far more nuance and explanation in a future article only focusing on the hierarchy of influences, this book humbly hints at how the disruptions in practice due to nonprofit journalism should impact how scholars of journalism studies theorize the hierarchy of influences model. The forces identified in this book influence this novel yet increasingly common market model's form of news production. However, these forces can be seen as a clear set of influences that can be applied to all kinds of journalism. In effect, this book's chapters can be viewed as a list of variables future scholars should use to understand why news looks the way it does across various market models. This manuscript also illustrates the ways in which the variables that have always influenced journalism in legacy news media continue to influence journalism at news nonprofits, just in different ways than before. In other words, the hierarchy of influences framework remains valuable and this book can be read as a persuasive argument in favor of its utility.

But, more germanely to this book, and the model, the social institutional level is considered more macro than the organizational level since the social institutional level fundamentally examines journalism's symbiotic relationship with other powerful institutions in society.[30] However, the majority of the institutions originally outlined as media influences – institutions such as the government, advertising, sources, the audience, public relations, etc. – originally impacted journalism organizations in a relatively similar manner. Prior to the many disruptions inherent in all forms of digital journalism, news organizations essentially looked the same, with similar reporting done by an advertising-funded model. Therefore, it made sense to theorize the social institutional level as something that impacts journalism organizations in a similar manner, to find that institutions such as the audience would exert relatively the same force on news construction across the media ecosystem.

Nonprofit journalism, though, illustrates the power of the organizational market model on journalistic practice. No more does the audience, for example, exert the same influence on all news organizations. As noted in this book, the vast majority of institutions influencing nonprofits do not do so in an equally distributed manner anymore. Nonprofit news organizations now have agency over how much and simply how these other intuitions impact their work. Whereas previously, institutions such as advertising impacted basically all news organizations, that is no longer the case; nonprofits have the ability to decide whether to accept advertising now. And, because advertising is now merely one stream of revenue amongst a far more diversified stream, it no longer has the same impact even if organizations accept it.

In a similar manner, foundation funding significantly affects journalism practice at nonprofits; these foundations, such as the Knight Foundation, are clearly other social institutions impacting journalism organizations. Each nonprofit studied for this book, though, engages with foundation support in a different way. A small number of nonprofits simply do not accept funding from these foundations. More frequently, though, nonprofits accept and seek out foundation funding. One editor relayed that when her organization is rewarded with foundation funding, the news organization and the funder will both sign a non-binding contract detailing how the news nonprofit retains all editorial control. This contract may eliminate direct editorial control from the funder, but the editor did not acknowledge that the funder relayed funds to impact coverage and news practice in a specific manner and therefore the funder enacts influence in a specific manner. Other journalists at nonprofits openly discussed chasing foundation funding, implicitly acknowledged that their organization would willingly alter journalistic practice if given the opportunity to receive funds.

In essence, the existing hierarchy of influences assumes that social institutions affect news organizations in a manner that leaves the news organization without much agency in the matter. This does not appear accurate anymore. For example, media ethics is often considered an industry-wide influence, something that does not differ from organization to organization. Scholars have argued that this influence occurs on the routines level and the social institution level. These ethics remain consistent across organizations and are embedded into journalistic routines, so much so that if an organization attempts to alter them, journalists will rebel.[31] Institutions such as the Society for Professional Journalists, universities and, on a more macro level, the government also impact the intersection of journalism and ethics.[32] Recent research concerning journalism in general illustrates how organizations now influence the application of media ethics – in some specific manners – more than any other level. For example, in photojournalism, professionals have argued that as recently as one decade ago, industry standards concerning ethical practices remained consistent across organizations, but due to emergent technology and organizational decisions, guidelines surrounding ethical practice vary from one news organization to the next.[33] In effect, while the industry essentially codified the practice of radical photo toning as unethical after the *Time* magazine controversy concerning a cover image of O.J. Simpson, today each news organization effectively implements its own policy on the practice. This anecdote can be extrapolated to nonprofit news organizations across a variety of influences from various social institutions.

Cumulatively, leadership decisions, market orientation, technology adoption and various other organizational factors influence how social institutions impact practice at news nonprofits. As previously mentioned, a nonprofit decides whether engagement is enough of a priority to incorporate platforms from, for example, Hearken, which then influences how journalists do their jobs. This decision, in a more comprehensive manner, illustrates how much the audience as a whole impacts practice. This is, again, an organizational decision. Therefore, this book exhibits data that supports the idea that the organizational level of analysis could reside above the social institutional level in the hierarchy of influences. While on the surface, the social institutional level is more macro than the organizational level, the way influence is manifest almost completely, now, relies on organizational decisions. Scholars consider communication routines more of a micro level than the organization even though these, theoretically, supersede organizational decision-making and exist across the industry. However, while social institutions previously exerted influence across the industry, that is no longer the case. These are now organizational differences, no different than technology adoption. Organizations have always decided whether to adopt technologies such as video, and now organizations decide whether to let social institutions such as advertising or foundations or the audience influence practice and at what level. Therefore, the findings in this book should and could begin a more rigorous and inclusive conversation about how the hierarchy of influences should function in an age of disruption and various market models.

Research on market models

While this book examines arguably the most prevalent journalism market model excluding legacy media solely funded by advertising, nonprofit journalism, its findings suggest that future work should acknowledge the power of market models in terms of their influence on journalistic practice. For more than a century, one market model dominated the journalism ecosystem. Now, nonprofit journalism – in its many incarnations – is just one of many disparate market models competing for citizens' attention. Prior research illustrates how market orientation can have significant effects on specific practices such as the incorporation of web analytics,[34] but an organization's market model supersedes market orientation. This book's data illustrate how the nonprofit market model is significantly disrupting digital journalism in numerous ways; therefore it is not hyperbole to suggest that other market models would have the same effect. This means that while current research in journalism studies often focuses on specific technologies such as analytics or recommender systems, thinking of these technologies as having the same affordances across organizations is myopic. An organization's market model will significantly influence how professional journalists utilize and perceive various technologies and other communication routines related to practice. In a sense, the organizational structure inherent in legacy media results a relatively stable set of influences on newswork, but new market models typically feature flattened organizational structures[35] that place far more power at the organizational level; this should result in more research on how market model impacts construction of news processes.

Conclusion

This book details the numerous ways in which nonprofit journalism disrupts digital journalism. In this time of industry upheaval and model experimentation, it is clear that nonprofit journalism is becoming the most popular and potentially – and relatively – sustainable funding model for journalism organizations. But changing how an organization is funded does not simply alter the newsroom's revenue stream; it significantly modifies virtually all aspects of news operation, primarily because of the multitude of previously existing and new influences applying force to journalistic practice.

While this work is absolutely not a total examination of the entire market model and certainly does not make a claim to have studied a census of United States-based digitally native news nonprofits, it is the most representative work looking at this model thus far. Other books detail the practices of one particular nonprofit,[36] or two works theoretically examine the potential effects nonprofit journalism can have on democracy,[37] but none focus on the actuality of how the model affects the newswork conducted by professional journalists, and none study as many organizations as represented here.

In its totality, the data analyzed for this book illustrate, beyond any doubt, that the nonprofit model is disrupting journalism. Some of the findings elucidate how practices at nonprofits are actually influencing how legacy media operate. For example, nonprofit journalism first began incorporating membership drives, but now legacy media are doing the same; the same can be said for foundation funds. In the end, it remains important to continue examining not only the influences affecting the growing field of digital nonprofit news, but also how nonprofit news is disrupting the ever-changing media ecosystem.

Notes

1 See Downie and Schudson, "The reconstruction of American journalism."
2 This statistic is courtesy of the Institute for Nonprofit News.
3 See Konieczna, *Journalism without profit* or Birnbauer, *The rise of nonprofit investigative journalism in the United States.*
4 For more on this, see Ferrucci, "Follow the leader."
5 See Ferrucci, "Murder incorporated" or "Primary differences."
6 See Kovach and Rosentiel, *The elements of journalism.*
7 See White, "The 'gate keeper.'"
8 See Shoemaker and Vos, *Gatekeeping theory.*
9 See Deuze, "The professional identity of journalists in the context of convergence culture."
10 See Ferrucci and Vos, "Who's in, who's out?"
11 See Vos and Ferrucci, "Who am I?"
12 See Klemm, Das and Hartmann, "Changed priorities ahead."
13 See Aitamurto and Varma, "The constructive role of journalism."
14 See Lewis, Holton and Coddington, "Reciprocal journalism."
15 See Groshek and Tandoc, "The affordance effect."
16 See Ferrucci, "Public journalism no more."
17 See Ferrucci, "Exploring public service journalism."
18 See Ferrucci, "Murder incorporated."
19 See Saltzis, "Breaking news online."

20 See Usher, "Venture-backed news startups and the field of journalism."
21 See Usher, "Newsroom moves and the newspaper crisis evaluated."
22 See Breed, "Social control in the newsroom."
23 See Schein, *Organizational culture and leadership.*
24 See Beam, "What it means to be a market-oriented newspaper."
25 See McManus, *Market-driven journalism.*
26 See Ferrucci, *It is in the numbers.*
27 See Baker, *Advertising and a democratic press.*
28 For arguments like this one, see Ferrucci, "Public journalism no more" or, more prominently, Konieczna, *Journalism without profit.*
29 See, for example, Coddington, "The wall becomes a curtain."
30 As noted throughout the book, for more on the model, see Shoemaker and Reese, *Mediating the message.*
31 See Ryfe, "Structure, agency, and change in an American newsroom" or *Can journalism survive?*
32 See Wilkins and Christians, *The handbook of mass media ethics.*
33 See Ferrucci and Taylor, "Blurred boundaries."
34 See Ferrucci, *It is in the numbers.*
35 For a more robust argument concerning the organizational level, see Ferrucci and Tandoc, "Shift in influence."
36 See Kennedy, *The wired city,* or Batsell, *Engaged journalism.*
37 See Konieczna, *Journalism without profit,* or Birnbauer, *The rise of nonprofit investigative journalism in the United States.*

Bibliography

Aitamurto, Tanja, and Anita Varma. 2018. "The constructive role of journalism: Contentious metadiscourse on constructive journalism and solutions journalism." *Journalism Practice* 12 (6): 695–713.

Baker, C. Edwin. 1994. *Advertising and a democratic press*. Princeton, NJ: Princeton University Press.

Barnouw, Erik, ed. 1997. *Conglomerates and the media*. New York: New Press.

Batsell, Jake. 2015. *Engaged journalism: Connecting with digitally empowered news audiences*. New York: Columbia University Press.

Beam, Randal A. 1998. "What it means to be a market-oriented newspaper." *Newspaper Research Journal* 19 (3): 2–20.

Beam, Randal A. 2003. "Content differences between daily newspapers with strong and weak market orientations." *Journalism & Mass Communication Quarterly* 80 (2): 368–390.

Belair-Gagnon, Valerie. 2015. *Social media at BBC news: The re-making of crisis reporting*. New York: Routledge.

Belair-Gagnon, Valerie. 2018. "News on the fly: Journalist-audience online engagement success as a cultural matching process." *Media, Culture & Society*: 0163443718813473.

Belair-Gagnon, Valerie, Jacob L. Nelson and Seth C. Lewis. 2018. "Audience engagement, reciprocity, and the pursuit of community connectedness in public media journalism." *Journalism Practice*: 10.1080/17512786. 2018.1542975.

Benson, Rodney. 2018. "Can foundations solve the journalism crisis?" *Journalism* 19 (8): 1059–1077.

Birnbauer, Bill. 2018. *The rise of nonprofit investigative journalism in the United States*. New York: Routledge.

Boorstin, Daniel J. 1961. *The image: A guide to pseudo-events in America*. New York: Vintage Books.

Breed, Warren. 1955. "Social control in the newsroom: A functional analysis." *Social Forces* 33 (4): 326–335.

Browne, Harry. 2010. "Foundation-funded journalism: Reasons to be wary of charitable support." *Journalism Studies* 11 (6): 889–903.

Carlson, Matt. 2015. "When news sites go native: Redefining the advertising–editorial divide in response to native advertising." *Journalism* 16 (7): 849–865.

Carlson, Matt. 2016. "Metajournalistic discourse and the meanings of journalism: Definitional control, boundary work, and legitimation." *Communication Theory* 26 (4): 349–368.

Carlson, Matt, and Nikki Usher. 2016. "News startups as agents of innovation: For-profit digital news startup manifestos as metajournalistic discourse." *Digital Journalism* 4 (5): 563–581.

Carpenter, Serena, Jan Boehmer and Frederick Fico. 2016. "The measurement of journalistic role enactments: A study of organizational constraints and support in for-profit and nonprofit journalism." *Journalism & Mass Communication Quarterly* 93 (3): 587–608.

Coddington, Mark. 2015. "The wall becomes a curtain: Revisiting journalism's news–business boundary." In *Boundaries of journalism: Professionalism, practices, and participation*, edited by Matt Carlson and Seth C. Lewis, 67–82. New York: Routledge.

Deuze, Mark. 2005. "What is journalism? Professional identity and ideology of journalists reconsidered." *Journalism* 6 (4): 442–464.

Deuze, Mark. 2008. "The professional identity of journalists in the context of convergence culture." *Observatorio (Obs*)* 2 (4): 103–117.

Djerf-Pierre, Monika. 2007. "The gender of journalism: The structure and logic of the field in the twentieth century." *Nordicom Review* 28: 81–104.

Downie, Leonard, and Michael Schudson. 2009. "The reconstruction of American journalism." *Columbia Journalism Review* (November/December), www.cjr.org/reconstruction/the_reconstruction_of_American.php.

Engelman, Ralph. 1996. *Public radio and television in America.* Thousand Oaks, CA: Sage.

Ferrucci, Patrick. 2015a. "Follow the leader: How leadership can affect the future of community journalism." *Community Journalism* 4 (2): 19–35.

Ferrucci, Patrick. 2015b. "Murder incorporated: Market orientation and coverage of the Annie Le Investigation." *Electronic News* 9 (2): 108–121.

Ferrucci, Patrick. 2015c. "Primary differences: How market orientation can influence content." *Journal of Media Practice* 16 (3): 195–210.

Ferrucci, Patrick. 2015d. "Public journalism no more: The digitally native news nonprofit and public service journalism." *Journalism* 16 (7): 904–919.

Ferrucci, Patrick. 2017a. "Exploring public service journalism: Digitally native news nonprofits and engagement." *Journalism & Mass Communication Quarterly* 94 (1): 355–370.

Ferrucci, Patrick. 2017b. "Technology allows audience role in news construction." *Newspaper Research Journal* 38 (1): 79–89.

Ferrucci, Patrick. 2018a. "Are You Experienced? How years in field affects digital journalists' perceptions of a changing industry." *Journalism Studies* 19 (16): 2417–2432.

Ferrucci, Patrick. 2018b. "It is in the numbers: How market orientation impacts journalists' use of news metrics." *Journalism*: 1464884918807056.

Ferrucci, Patrick. 2018c. "Money matters? Journalists' perception of the effects of a weak market orientation." *Convergence* 24 (4): 424–438.

Ferrucci, Patrick. 2018d. "Networked: Social media's impact on news production in digital newsrooms." *Newspaper Research Journal* 39 (1): 6–17.

Ferrucci, Patrick. 2018e. ""We've lost the basics": Perceptions of journalism education from veterans in the field." *Journalism & Mass Communication Educator* 73 (4): 410–420.

Ferrucci, Patrick, and Kathleen I. Alaimo. In press. "Escaping the news desert: Nonprofit news and open-system journalism organizations." *Journalism*.

Ferrucci, Patrick, and Edson C. Tandoc Jr. 2015. "A tale of two newsrooms: How market orientation affects web analytics use." In *Contemporary research methods and data analytics in the news industry*, edited by William Gibbs and Joseph McKendrick, 58–76. Philadelphia, PA: IGI Global.

Ferrucci, Patrick, and Edson C. Tandoc Jr. 2017. "Shift in influence: An argument for changes in studying gatekeeping." *Journal of Media Practice* 18 (2–3): 103–119.

Ferrucci, Patrick, and Ross Taylor. 2019. "Blurred boundaries: Toning ethics in news routines." *Journalism Studies*: 10.1080/1461670X.2019.1577165.

Ferrucci, Patrick, and Tim Vos. 2017. "Who's in, who's out? Constructing the identity of digital journalists." *Digital Journalism* 5 (7): 868–883.

Fishman, Mark. 1988. *Manufacturing the news*. Austin, TX: University of Texas Press.

Gans, Herbert J. 1979. *Deciding what's news: A study of CBS evening news, NBC nightly news, Newsweek, and Time*. New York: Pantheon Books.

Graves, Lucas. 2016. *Deciding what's true: The rise of political fact-checking in American journalism*. New York: Columbia University Press.

Groves, Jonathan, and Carrie Brown. 2011. "Stopping the presses: A longitudinal case study of the Christian Science Monitor transition from print daily to web always." International Symposium on Online Journalism.

Groshek, Jacob, and Edson C. Tandoc. 2017. "The affordance effect: Gatekeeping and (non) reciprocal journalism on Twitter." *Computers in Human Behavior* 66: 201–210.

Jaakkola, Maarit, Heikki Hellman, Kari Koljonen and Jari Väliverronen. 2015. "Liquid modern journalism with a difference: The changing professional ethos of cultural journalism." *Journalism Practice* 9 (6): 811–828.

Janis, Irving Lester. 1982. *Groupthink: Psychological studies of policy decisions and fiascoes*. Boston, MA: Houghton Mifflin.

Jian, Lian, and Nikki Usher. 2014. "Crowd-funded journalism." *Journal of Computer-Mediated Communication* 19 (2): 155–170.

Kaye, Jeff, and Stephen Quinn. 2010. *Funding journalism in the digital age: Business models, strategies, issues and trends*. New York: Peter Lang.

Kennedy, Dan. 2013. *The wired city: Reimagining journalism and civic life in the post-newspaper age*. Amherst, MA: University of Massachusetts Press.

Klemm, Celine, Enny Das and Tilo Hartmann. 2017. "Changed priorities ahead: Journalists' shifting role perceptions when covering public health crises." *Journalism*: 1464884917692820.

Konieczna, Magda. 2014. "Do old norms have a place in new media? A case study of the nonprofit MinnPost." *Journalism Practice* 8 (1): 49–64.

Konieczna, Magda. 2018. *Journalism without profit: Making news when the market fails*. New York: Oxford University Press.

Konieczna, Magda, and Elia Powers. 2017. "What can nonprofit journalists actually do for democracy?" *Journalism Studies* 18 (12): 1542–1558.

Kopytowska, Monika Weronika, and Yusuf Kalyango. 2013. *Why discourse matters: Negotiating identity in the mediatized world*. New York: Peter Lang

Kovach, Bill, and Tom Rosenstiel. 2007. *The elements of journalism: What newspeople should know and the public should expect*. New York: Three Rivers Press.

Larson, Christine. 2015. "Live publishing: The onstage redeployment of journalistic authority." *Media, Culture & Society* 37 (3): 440–459.

Lewis, Justin, and Stephen Cushion. 2009. "The thirst to be first: An analysis of breaking news stories and their impact on the quality of 24-hour news coverage in the UK." *Journalism Practice* 3 (3): 304–318.

Lewis, Seth C. 2011. "Journalism innovation and participation: An analysis of the Knight News Challenge." *International Journal of Communication* 5 (2011): 1623–1648.

Lewis, Seth C., Avery E. Holton and Mark Coddington. 2014. "Reciprocal journalism: A concept of mutual exchange between journalists and audiences." *Journalism Practice* 8 (2): 229–241.

Lowrey, Wilson, Lindsey Sherrill and Ryan Broussard. 2019. "Field and ecology approaches to journalism innovation: The role of ancillary organizations." *Journalism Studies* : 1–19.

McChesney, Robert W., and John Nichols. 2011. *The death and life of American journalism: The media revolution that will begin the world again*. New York: Nation Books.

McDevitt, Michael, and Patrick Ferrucci. 2018. "Populism, journalism, and the limits of reflexivity: The case of Donald J. Trump." *Journalism Studies* 19 (4): 512–526.

McDevitt, Michael, and Shannon Sindorf. 2012. "How to kill a journalism school: The digital sublime in the discourse of discontinuance." *Journalism & Mass Communication Educator* 67 (2): 109–118.

McManus, John H. 1994. *Market-driven journalism: Let the citizen beware?* Thousand Oaks, CA: Sage Publications.

Nee, Rebecca Coates. 2013. "Creative destruction: An exploratory study of how digitally native news nonprofits are innovating online journalism practices." *International Journal on Media Management* 15 (1): 3–22.

Nee, Rebecca Coates. 2014. "Social responsibility theory and the digital nonprofits: Should the government aid online news startups?" *Journalism* 15 (3): 326–343.

Nelson, Jacob L. 2018. "And deliver us to segmentation: The growing appeal of the niche news audience." *Journalism Practice* 12 (2): 204–219.

Nelson, Jacob L. 2018. "The elusive engagement metric." *Digital Journalism* 6 (4): 528–544.

Nelson, Jacob L., and Edson C. Tandoc Jr. "Doing 'well' or doing 'good': What audience analytics reveal about journalism's competing goals." *Journalism Studies*: 10.1080/1461670X.2018.1547122.

Painter, Chad E., and Patrick Ferrucci. 2018. "Digital marketplace: The influence of market forces on normative role in the Internet age." In *Ethics for a Digital Age, Vol II*, edited by Donald Heider and Bastiaan Vanacker, 109–124. New York: Peter Lang.

Palmer, Ruth. 2017. *Becoming the news: How ordinary people respond to the media spotlight.* New York: Columbia University Press.

Peters, Jonathan, and Edson C. Tandoc. 2013. "'People who aren't really reporters at all, who have no professional qualifications': Defining a journalist and deciding who may claim the privileges." *NYU Journal of Legislation and Public Policy* 34: 34–63

Phillips, Angela. 2010. "Transparency and the new ethics of journalism." *Journalism Practice* 4 (3): 373–382.

Powers, Elia, and Ronald A. Yaros. 2012. "Supporting online nonprofit news organizations: Do financial contributions influence stakeholder expectations and engagement?" *Journal of Media Business Studies* 9 (3): 41–62.

Powers, Elia, and Ronald A. Yaros. 2013. "Cultivating support for nonprofit news organizations: commitment, trust and donating audiences." *Journal of Communication Management* 17 (2): 157–170.

Reese, Stephen D. 2001. "Understanding the global journalist: A hierarchy-of-influences approach." *Journalism Studies* 2 (2): 173–187.

Reese, Stephen D., and Pamela J. Shoemaker. 2016. "A media sociology for the networked public sphere: The hierarchy of influences model." *Mass Communication and Society* 19 (4): 389–410.

Rosen, Jay. 1996. *Getting the connections right: Public journalism and the troubles in the press.* New York: Twentieth Century Fund.

Rosen, Jay. 1999. *What are journalists for?* New Haven, CT: Yale University Press.

Russell, Frank Michael. 2016. "Silicon Valley and the new gatekeepers: an institutional view of journalism, technology, and social sharing of news." Dissertation, University of Missouri–Columbia.

Ryfe, David M. 2009. "Structure, agency, and change in an American newsroom." *Journalism* 10 (5): 665–683.

Ryfe, David M. 2013. *Can journalism survive?: An inside look at American newsrooms.* New York: John Wiley & Sons.

Saltzis, Kostas. 2012. "Breaking news online: How news stories are updated and maintained around-the-clock." *Journalism Practice* 6 (5–6): 702–710.

Schauster, Erin E., Patrick Ferrucci and Marlene S. Neill. 2016. "Native advertising is the new journalism: How deception affects social responsibility." *American Behavioral Scientist* 60 (12): 1408–1424.

Schein, Edgar H. 2006. *Organizational culture and leadership.* San Francisco, CA: Jossey-Bass.

Schudson, Michael. 2001. "The objectivity norm in American journalism." *Journalism* 2 (2): 149–170.

Schudson, Michael. 2003. *The sociology of news:* New York: Norton.

Sherwood, Merryn, and Penny O'Donnell. 2018. "Once a journalist, always a journalist? Industry restructure, job loss and professional identity." *Journalism Studies* 19 (7): 1021–1038.

Shoemaker, Pamela J., and Stephen D. Reese. 2014. *Mediating the message in the 21st century: A media sociology perspective*. New York: Routledge.

Shoemaker, Pamela J., and Tim P. Vos. 2009. *Gatekeeping theory*. New York: Routledge.

Tandoc Jr, Edson C. 2014. "Journalism is twerking? How web analytics is changing the process of gatekeeping." *New Media & Society* 16 (4): 559–575.

Tandoc Jr, Edson C., Lea Hellmueller and Tim P. Vos. 2013. "Mind the gap: Between journalistic role conception and role enactment." *Journalism Practice* 7 (5): 539–554.

Tandoc Jr, Edson C., Zheng Wei Lim and Richard Ling. 2018. "Defining 'fake news': A typology of scholarly definitions." *Digital Journalism* 6 (2): 137–153.

Tuchman, Gaye. 1978. *Making news: A study in the construction of reality*. New York: Free Press.

Usher, Nikki. 2015. "Newsroom moves and the newspaper crisis evaluated: Space, place, and cultural meaning." *Media, Culture & Society* 37 (7): 1005–1021.

Usher, Nikki. 2017. "Venture-backed news startups and the field of journalism: Challenges, changes, and consistencies." *Digital Journalism* 5 (9): 1116–1133.

Van Zoonen, Liesbet. 2002. "One of the girls?: The changing gender of journalism." In *News, gender and power*, edited by Stuart Allen, Gill Branston and Cynthia Carter, 45–58. New York: Routledge.

Vos, Tim P. 2019. "Journalists' endangered professional status." *Journalism* 20 (1): 122–125.

Vos, Tim P., Stephanie Craft and Seth Ashley. 2012. "New media, old criticism: Bloggers' press criticism and the journalistic field." *Journalism* 13 (7): 850–868.

Vos, Tim P., and Patrick Ferrucci. 2018. "Who am I? Perceptions of digital journalists' professional identity." In *The Routledge Handbook of Developments in Digital Journalism Studies*, edited by Scott Eldridge II and Bob Franklin, 40–52. New York: Routledge.

Vos, Tim P., and François Heinderyckx. 2015. *Gatekeeping in transition*. New York: Routledge.

Weaver, David Hugh, Randal A. Beam, Bonnie J. Brownlee, Paul Voakes and G. Cleveland Wilhoit. 2007. *The American journalist in the 21st century: US news people at the dawn of a new millennium*. New York: Routledge.

Weaver, David Hugh, and G. Cleveland Wilhoit. 1991. *The American journalist: A portrait of US news people and their work*. Bloomington, IN: Indiana University Press.

Weaver, David Hugh, and G. Cleveland Wilhoit. 1996. *The American journalist in the 1990s: US news people at the end of an era*. Mahwah, NJ: Erlbaum.

White, David Manning. 1950. "The 'gate keeper': A case study in the selection of news." *Journalism Quarterly* 27: 383–390.

Wilkins, Lee, and Clifford G. Christians. 2008. *The handbook of mass media ethics*. New York: Routledge.

Willnat, Lars, David Hugh Weaver, and G. Cleveland Wilhoit. 2017. *The American journalist in the digital age: A half-century perspective*. New York: Peter Lang.

Index